Industrial Archaeology

For the industrial archaeologist the Midlands is the most exciting region of all. It was the cradle of Britain's industrial revolution and the evidence is here for all to see. From the abundant relics of the region's industrial past, the author has carefully selected a wide range of examples, illustrating how an archaeologist today can re-create a detailed picture of this period.

Industrial archaeology is not just a study of museums and excavations but is also the understanding of artefacts of the late eighteenth and nineteenth centuries. In pointing out the factories, foundries, workshops and manufacturers' houses, the author explains the development from village craft to factory. We are thus helped to more fully examine today's evidence of this most vital period of Midland history.

The story is of Midland men, machinery and buildings – from the Shropshire iron-masters and the great iron bridge at Coalbrookdale, to Boulton and Watt's steam-engine; from the forges and slitting mills of the River Stour, to the lace industries of Nottingham and Leicester; from boots and shoes in Northamptonshire to Black Country nail and chain making and to brewing in Burton.

The book contains more than forty photographs and line drawings, a glossary and index.

(Editor)

WAYLAND REGIONAL STUDIES

THE MIDLANDS

Industrial Archaeology

Geoffrey Booth

WAYLAND PUBLISHERS LONDON

More Midland Books

Frontispiece: Crowds gather after a
fatal explosion at Bunker's-Hill
Mine, in North Staffordshire.

SBN 85340 319 8
Copyright © 1973 by Wayland (Publishers) Ltd
101 Grays Inn Road London WC1
Printed in Great Britain by
The Garden City Press Limited
Letchworth, Hertfordshire SG6 1JS

Contents

List of Illustrations

Introduction

If any region can claim to be the cradle of the Industrial Revolution, it is the Midlands. It is important to remember, however, that some of the greatest Midlands industrialists were Midlanders not by birth but by adoption. For example Richard Arkwright, cotton spinner, moved to Nottingham from Lancashire. So did Hargreaves, inventor of the spinning jenny. John Wilkinson, iron master, moved from north Lancashire to Bersham, near Wrexham, then to Shropshire and finally south to Staffordshire. And James Watt moved from Glasgow to Birmingham to join Matthew Boulton, a native industrialist.

Yet, while these industrialists were at work – building machines, developing smelting with coal and improving the steam engine – nails, chains and other goods continued to be produced in the Black Country by the old methods of hand forging in the small domestic workshop. In fact in numerical terms, over Britain as a whole, the village craftsman was the typical producer during the Industrial Revolution. Throughout the eighteenth century and for part of the nineteenth, thousands earned their livelihood as framework knitters or lace makers in the east Midlands and as chain, nail, toy, needle, silk ribbon and watchmakers in the west Midlands.

The factory system first developed using the traditional sources of power – wind, animals and water. Derbyshire cotton spinners, for example, quickly utilized the water power of the River Derwent. The River Stour had numerous forges and slitting mills along it, while the Alne and the Arrow drove many needle mills. And corn was ground in small, rural wind and water mills all over the region. The Black Country, Birmingham and Nottingham, however, were not well supplied with water power. So, in these places, power was provided by animals – the machinery at Ark-

Opposite Cressbrook Mill in Derbyshire. This was built in 1815.

8

wright's factory at Nottingham, for instance, was driven by horses.

The Midlands was the first region to exploit Newcomen's atmospheric steam engine in the coal and lead mines, and these were later used in factories throughout the region. The great Boulton and Watt partnership in Birmingham produced steam engines for the world, and Soho became a name associated with high quality engineering.

In a book of this length, however, it is impossible to cover all aspects of industrial archaeology and there are necessarily some omissions. The most obvious of these is transport, which has probably received the greatest attention from other writers and which is covered in another book in this series. The topics which have been selected for this volume have been studied with reference to one or two Midland examples – for to attempt a blanket survey in every part of the Midlands would be so general that it would be virtually meaningless. Nevertheless, the local events have been related to the wider Midlands, as well as the national, patterns of industry.

Below A typical courtyard pottery factory in the late eighteenth century.

Mineral Wealth – Coal

By the middle of the nineteenth century there were nearly four hundred collieries in the Black Country alone and, in 1855, the Leicester, Derbyshire and Nottinghamshire coalfields were producing nearly $3\frac{1}{2}$ million tons of coal a year. There were also especially good coal seams in east Shropshire and south Staffordshire, where the famous Ten Yard seam stretched in an arc from Dudley, through Tipton, to Bilston and Wednesbury. This was one of the richest and thickest seams in the whole country. As early as 1725 there were over fifty collieries along the eastern edge of the east Warwickshire coalfield, which runs from Tamworth to Coventry. There were thick seams in this field but, because they dipped steeply, drainage was a considerable problem. In the east Midlands coal was mined around Coleorton and Measham, and a map of Leicestershire shows thirty-eight collieries in existence in 1775.

The exploitation of these coal measures had an enormous impact on the Midlands region. The lead was taken by the owners of landed estates. Sir Roger Newdigate, for example, began to exploit the coal-measures on his estate at Arbury (near Nuneaton) in the seventeenth century. But few colliery proprietors could afford to develop all the promising parts of their estates at once. So they chose the area which appeared to have the greatest potential for development and then rented other parts of the field to local men. They retained, however, overall control of mining methods. At their Griff colliery, the Newdigate family was in the forefront of mining technology. Huts and cottages were built for the miners and, because local skilled labour proved insufficient, a number of recruiting agents were sent to Shropshire between 1701 and 1729. A total of 171 people were employed at the colliery in 1701. These included young boys, who worked underground as well

PLACES TO VISIT

Bedworth, Warwickshire – a colliery town.

Coalville, Leicestershire – housing and colliery office.

Cinderhill, Nottingham – colliery housing.

10

as driving the *gin horses*, operating air pumps and acting as *balers*, and women who were all given surface jobs – such as riddling coal. Griff colliery has only recently been closed and spoil tips still remain. Although no eighteenth century colliers' houses have survived, Bedworth has all the appearances of a nineteenth century mining town.

Another landed family that exploited its mineral rights were the Earls of Dudley. They took less personal responsibility for their mines than the Newdigates and relied heavily on land agents and mining engineers to manage their enterprises. In 1797 a skilled engineer, C. Beaumont, was brought from Newcastle to reorganize Viscount Dudley's pits. Beaumont felt that his duties included "raising the greatest quantity and on the lowest terms . . . simplifying a work of such vast extension so as to prevent imposition . . . and above all to . . . produce an immense revenue." By 1833 the Dudleys had a gross income of £117,493 per year; and the estate owned and managed ten large collieries, a clay pit, extensive limestone mines, three iron works, two store yards, a mineral railway, and many cottages and farms.

Left Newcomen's atmospheric pumping engine at Griff colliery, from an engraving by Henry Beighton (1717).

Mining methods

Methods of mining depended in part on the accessibility of the coalmeasures. Remains of *bell pits* – the most primitive method of mining – can still be seen in parts of Leicestershire and Shropshire. But by the middle of the eighteenth century the *longwall system*, thought to have originated in Shropshire, had spread through most of the Midlands. By this method the coal is extracted in one operation. The works advance in a continuous line and the space previously occupied by coal is filled in with stones and refuse. In contrast, in the North Eastern Coalfield, the *pillar and stall* method was used almost everywhere.

These differences in mining methods also included the organization of mining. In the Midlands, particularly in Staffordshire, a form of subcontracting – known as the *butty system* – was operated. The workmen at the coal face were not paid by the owner of the colliery but by a contractor, the butty. The butty was neither a mining engineer nor a manager, but a working collier who had "a knowledge of the business" and "an acquaintance with the habits of the men." He agreed to produce coal or ironstone from the mine at a fixed price per ton, and he himself hired and paid the labour and supplied the necessary tools. Under this system the men were overworked and the smaller collieries were exploited for short-term profit.

The butty system grew stronger in the Midlands towards the end of the nineteenth century, as the Ten Yard seam was worked out and operations shifted to thinner seams. The survival of this system, which had died out in most other areas in the early eighteenth century, is less surprising if one looks at the Black Country coal industry within the wider context of the west Midlands craft industries. Here the small master was a dominant character and subcontracting was common.

PLACES TO VISIT

Dudley Library and Museum – photographs of the Black Country.

Nuneaton area and Cannock area – spoil tips, pithead winding gear.

Above A coal pit worked by women.

Opposite The Midlands coalfields.

The Staffordshire coal industry has been declining throughout the twentieth century and even that characteristic physical sign of mining, the pit-head winding gear, is fast disappearing. The tips become grassed over as they have near Nuneaton – where they could, with some justification, be called the Nuneaton Alps.

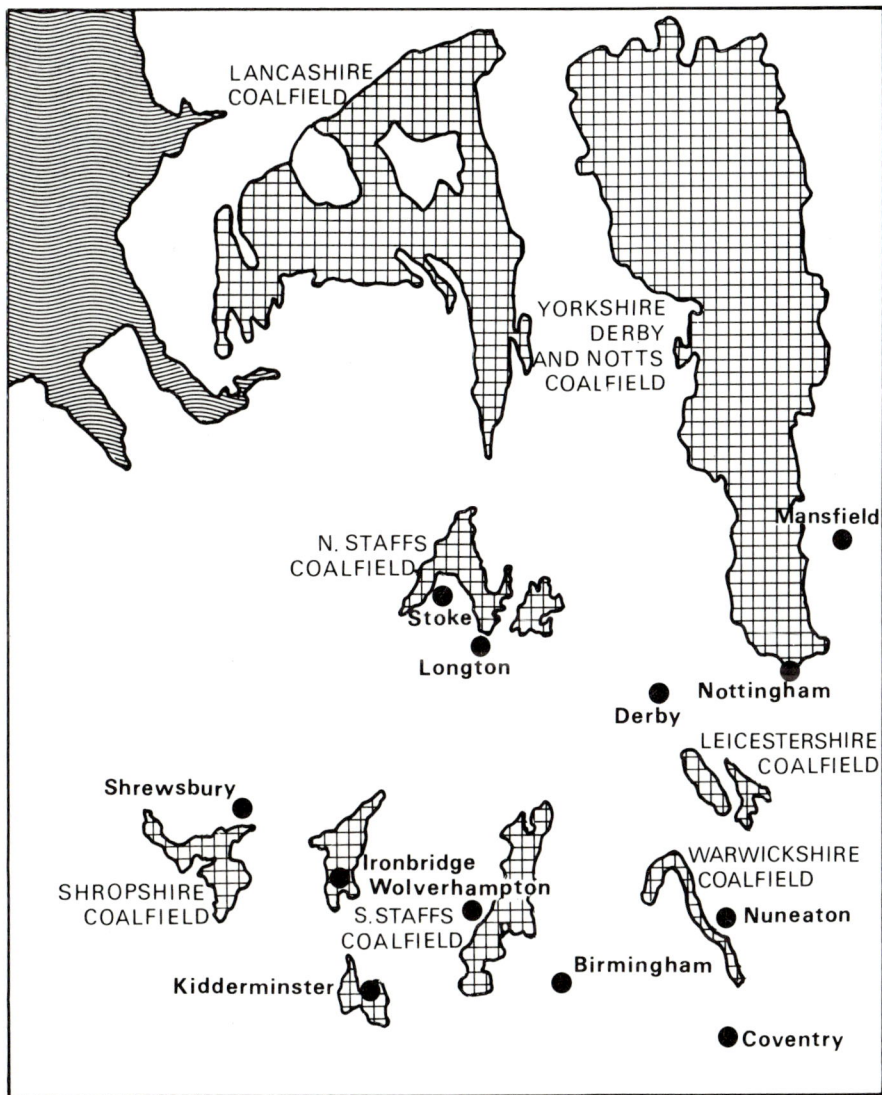

LANCASHIRE
COALFIELD

YORKSHIRE
DERBY
AND NOTTS
COALFIELD

N. STAFFS
COALFIELD

Mansfield

Stoke

Longton

Nottingham

Derby

LEICESTERSHIRE
COALFIELD

Shrewsbury

WARWICKSHIRE
COALFIELD

SHROPSHIRE
COALFIELD

Ironbridge
Wolverhampton

Nuneaton

S.STAFFS
COALFIELD

Kidderminster

Birmingham

Coventry

Drainage

The landed proprietors of the west Midlands were quick to adopt improved power systems for mine drainage. In 1712, Lord Dudley installed the first Newcomen steam engine to drain the Coneygree coal mine at Tipton. In 1714, the second Newcomen engine was installed at the Griff colliery. Another was installed about 1717. By 1733, there were at least thirty Newcomen engines in the Midlands coalfields. The majority of these were in Staffordshire and Warwickshire. No buildings associated with these early engines are known to survive, but drawings amongst the Newdigate papers show them to have been simple, two storey, stone buildings, from which one end of the beam with the pump rod projected.

During the eighteenth century Newcomen engines were erected in increasing numbers. There were at least twenty-five in the Derbyshire coalfield for example. Some of the later Derbyshire engines were built by Francis Thompson of Ashover. In 1791, he erected an engine at Oakerthorpe colliery and the ruined engine house still survives. The engine was saved and can be seen at the Science Museum in London.

Drainage had been a persistent problem in the Warwickshire coalfield. As early as 1705 a map shows horse gins, water wheels and a windmill all operating pumps or buckets to raise water. Horse gins and water wheels were also used for coal drawing and, in 1774, the Newdigates installed a Smeaton water wheel for this purpose. Horse gins were widely used in the east Midlands. One from Pinxton Green Colliery, in Derbyshire, has been removed for preservation by the National Coal Board. It is now at the colliery training school at Bentinck.

Boulton and Watt engines were used solely for pumping until 1781, when Watt developed rotary power. Their first engine was installed at Bloomfield Colliery,

PLACES TO VISIT

Soho Foundry, Smethwick – old foundry buildings, housing built by Boulton and Watt.

Oakerthorpe, Derbyshire – engine house.

Bentinck Colliery Training School, Derbyshire – winding gin.

Tipton. But Boulton and Watt engines were much more expensive than Newcomen engines. Their main advantage was that they used less fuel, but this was largely irrelevant to a colliery proprietor and Newcomen engines continued to be more popular.

The first Newcomen and Boulton and Watt engines, therefore, were erected at Midlands collieries. The first railway in Britain was also laid in a Midland coal mine. Huntingdon Beaumont, having learnt something of German mining technology, installed a railway system in the pits belonging to the Willoughbys in Nottinghamshire in 1603–4. The greatest development of wooden railways took place in the north-east, but they were also constructed extensively in Shropshire during the eighteenth century and carried coal from the pits to ironworks at Severnside. The routes of many of them can be traced on the ground.

The coming of the railways to the Midlands provided opportunities for the exploitation of parts of the coalfields that were not served by the canal system. The east Midlands had been less well off in this respect than the west Midlands. Extensive developments now took place in Leicestershire, Nottinghamshire and the Cannock area of Staffordshire. Housing was provided at a number of sites. Thomas North, for example, took leases of 9,500 acres of coalfield to the west of Nottingham, and much of the housing in Cinderhill was built by him.

Above The later Boulton and Watt engines which were erected at Midlands collieries were made at the Soho Foundry in Birmingham. The Foundry was built in 1795–96 and was later owned by W. & T. Avery, scales manufacturers.

Right A contemporary sketch of Griff colliery in the eighteenth century, showing atmospheric pumping engines and coal boats.

Iron

The exploitation of coal was closely linked with that of iron in the eighteenth and nineteenth centuries. Ironstone generally occurred in nodules and bands in the coalmeasures. Landed proprietors who developed their mineral resources, like the Earls of Dudley, were also often involved in the setting up of ironworks. But the quality of the ore varied over the region. Some of the highest quality was in Shropshire. Until 1709 in theory, and in practice until after about 1750, ironmasters were dependent upon charcoal for smelting. Furnaces, therefore, had to be located near plentiful supplies of coppice wood. Even so, there was a considerable trade in charcoal and some ironmasters had to obtain it from a number of sites within a radius of about twenty miles from their furnaces. Water power was required to operate the bellows, which provided blast for the furnace and power for the hammers.

The *pig iron* or forged bars had to be transported to market and the River Severn was the great natural highway for the west Midlands. This enabled Shropshire ironmasters to have close links with Bristol. Canal links with the Severn were particularly important to merchants in the Birmingham area, and to the owners of the numerous forges along the edge of the Black Country. The Moira Ironworks in Leicestershire were built in 1804 when the Ashby Canal was opened, and the existence of the Trent and its canal links with Chesterfield was vitally important to the Derbyshire iron industry. The new south Staffordshire ironworks, which were built in the nineteenth century, were situated close to the existing canal system. And, when the Northamptonshire ores were developed, railway communication was vital. Many factors, therefore, influenced the location of the iron industry.

Whereas the exploitation of a small coal pit required little capital, the building and operation of a charcoal

PLACES TO VISIT

Moira, Leicestershire –
blast furnaces.

Ironbridge Gorge Museum –
Bedlam furnaces.

Ironbridge, Shropshire – the
iron bridge.

or coke blast furnace required considerably more. For this reason, many of the eighteenth and early nineteenth century furnaces were operated by ironmasters in partnership. The Horsehay Works in Shropshire had two partners while Lightmoor Ironworks, set up between 1755 and 1758, had ten. New Willey had eleven partners and the Madeley Wood Furnaces had thirteen. Not all these partners were local men – one came from Evesham, and six of the New Willey partners were Bristol men. Neither were they all directly involved in the iron industry – all the Bristol partners were merchants, there was a Shrewsbury draper and several "gentlemen." During the last third of the eighteenth century the Shropshire iron industry was dominated by men of exceptional ability: John Wilkinson, Richard and William Reynolds, John Onions, Francis Homfray and the Darby family. Abraham Darby III rebuilt the old furnace in 1777 in order to cast the parts of the iron bridge which was erected across the Severn between 1777 and 1779 – the first iron bridge in the world. This and other important remains of Shropshire's iron industry are now preserved as part of the Ironbridge Gorge Museum.

Left The first iron bridge in the world was erected across the River Severn, near Broseley, between 1777 and 1779. It was cast at the Coalbrookdale iron works by Abraham Darby III.

17

Ironworks

Charcoal blast furnaces were either circular or square in cross section, with a cylindrical inner casing from the mid-seventeenth century. There were holes for the tuyeres (nozzles of the bellows) and a hearth in front of the furnace for casting. Fuel and ironstone were loaded in at the top and the metal was tapped near the base of the furnace. One of the most complete charcoal blast furnaces in Britain survives at Charlcotte, in Shropshire. Where no structure survives one of the first indications of iron working is the existence of slag. It is possible to identify charcoal furnace slag quite easily. It is dark and glassy in appearance, with bubbles in it. It is also heavy, which indicates that not all the metal was removed during smelting. Another clue to the existence of furnace and forge sites is a chain of pools or mill ponds. For most other industrial processes one mill pond was enough, but so much power was needed in smelting and forging that it is quite usual to find two or even three ponds at the site of an old iron works.

After the iron had been smelted it was sent to a forge to be made into bars, rods or other goods. The forge consisted of a range of low buildings containing hearths and tilt hammers. Here the pig iron was remelted, refined and hammered. The slitting mill was another type of iron works, which had been introduced in Britain in the sixteenth century. Here iron was rolled and slit into rods for chain, nail and other small metal manufacturers. The furnace, forge and slitting mill all required power. The different operations, therefore, were usually carried out at different sites so that each could have sufficient power. The slitting mill, since it was not so closely tied to supplies of iron as the forge, tended to be situated nearer to the customer. The Worcestershire Stour probably had more slitting mills along it than any other river in England in the seventeenth and eighteenth centuries.

Above The Phoenix Foundry in Birmingham.

PLACES TO VISIT

Charlcotte, Shropshire – charcoal blast furnace.

Willey, near Broseley – chain of mill pools, slag heaps at site of John Wilkinson's iron works.

Ironville, near Ripley – industrial village built by the Butterley Company.

The search for power and raw materials often led the ironmaster to establish his works some distance from a source of labour. He had, therefore, to build houses for his workers. Good examples can be seen in many parts of Shropshire, although demolition has removed some in recent years. One of the most interesting sites is at Eardington Lower Forge, south of Bridgnorth. Nearly all the industrial settlements belong to the water power age, but there is one important exception – Ironville. This was built between 1825 and 1850 by the Butterley Company, Derbyshire, and is a complete township on a larger scale than the water power industrial sites. It heralds Saltaire in Yorkshire or Port Sunlight in Cheshire.

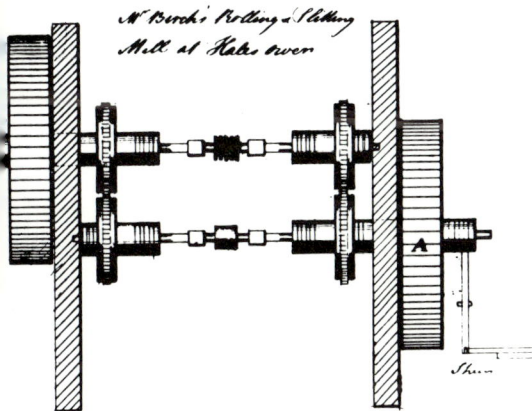

Above An early drawing showing the cross-section of Mr. Birch's rolling and slitting mill at Halesowen.

FURNACES IN THE MIDLANDS 1717

County	Furnace	Output (tons) p.a.
Derbyshire	Staveley	150
	Foxbrook	150
	Wingerworth	200
	Wanley	300
Herefordshire	St. Waynards	300
	Bringewood	450
	Bishopswood	600
Nottinghamshire	Kirby	200
Shropshire	Charlcotte	400
	Bouldon	400
	Coalbrookdale	250
	Leighton	400
	Kimberton	250
	Willey	450
	Madeley	400
Staffordshire	Merheath	600
	Grange	450
Warwickshire	Aston	400
	Pool Bank	300
Worcestershire	Cradley	200
	Halesowen	500

Smelting with coke

With the increase in the number of furnaces and forges the reserves of coppice wood began to be severely strained. Since the seventeenth century, ironmasters had been attempting to find a method of smelting with coal or coke. In 1665, Dud Dudley claimed to have achieved success. No documentary evidence in support of Dud Dudley's claim has been found but, a few years ago, lumps of slag taken from the site of his works at Himley, Staffordshire, were found to contain large pieces of coke.

The first successful use of coke in smelting was achieved by Abraham Darby I at Coalbrookdale, in 1709. Although Darby did not patent his discoveries, it was not until the 1750s that other ironmasters began to adopt the process. By 1759 there were twelve coke furnaces in Shropshire, and many more were built during the 1770s. In 1788, there were twenty-one coke and three charcoal furnaces producing about 24,900 tons a year – approximately 37 per cent of the total British output. And in 1800 Telford, the engineer, remarked that: "The number of blast furnaces for iron between Ketley and Willey (Salop) exceeds any within the same space in the kingdom."

The adoption of coke smelting prompted the ironmasters to build new furnaces within easy access of good supplies of coal. In Shropshire there was a shift to the east side of the Severn. In Derbyshire, where the first coke furnace had been built in 1780, the coke smelting industry was firmly located along the coal measures in the east of the county. In Staffordshire, the Bradley iron works were set up near Bilston by John Wilkinson and, by 1800, there were about twenty-six blast furnaces in the Black Country. Most of them were located along the canals in the area between Bilston, Wednesbury and Dudley.

By 1806 the Shropshire iron industry was past its

PLACES TO VISIT

Ironbridge Gorge Museum – Coalbrookdale furnaces and company museum.

Morley Park blast furnaces, Derbyshire.

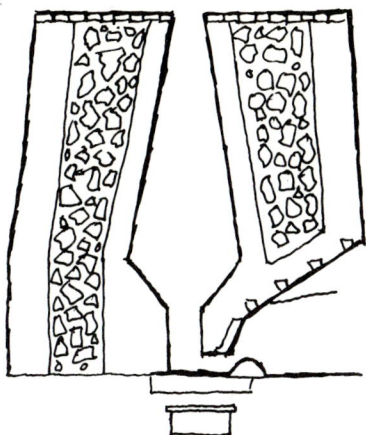

Above A cross-section of a blast furnace.

Below Cold-blast iron furnaces at Morley Park, built in 1780 and 1818.

peak. Ironmasters and capital flowed to south Wales and south Staffordshire. The main reason for this seems to have been its remoteness from the important market of the west Midlands and the ports, as well as a failure to employ new machines and processes and to make new products. Shropshire now became an industrial backwater and this explains why the county has so many remains of its iron industry.

Ironfounding and general engineering were far more widespread than the production of pig iron. The establishment of large works demanded adequate transport for raw materials and the works in Northampton were all set up after the completion of the branch canal in 1815. There were fifteen foundries in the town in the early nineteenth century. Numerous forges and foundries were also established in the Black Country as the market for domestic stoves, kitchen ranges, piping, water systems and ornamental furniture increased. Cast iron mileposts were made for local turnpike trusts and many can be seen on the roads radiating from Derby. The gas industry provided another outlet for the products of local foundries. The industrial archaeologist will find more evidence of these firms' activities in their products – such as gratings, man-hole covers, street lamps, letter boxes, grates and cooking ranges – than at the site at which they were produced.

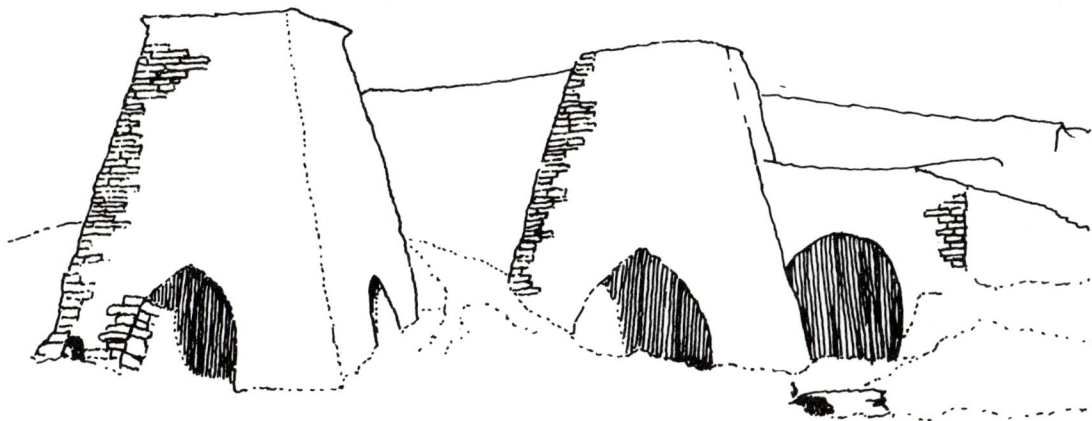

Lead

There were two important lead mining areas in the Midlands – central Derbyshire and south Shropshire. In both areas mining occurred intermittently after the Roman occupation, but during the eighteenth century the Derbyshire mines were developed on a much larger scale than those in Shropshire. Lead mining in Derbyshire was subject to ancient laws and customs. Anyone had the right to mine in these areas, so long as he paid the owner of the mineral rights a percentage of the profits in kind. In Shropshire, on the other hand, the landowner leased a mine to an individual or a company for a certain number of years. During the early eighteenth century, mining was generally carried out by small groups of men who dug shallow shafts in the veins. The hummocks and hollows above Wirksworth, Brassington and Winster in Derbyshire are the surface remains of these activities. The Derbyshire miners built single storey huts, called *coes*, in which they stored their tools and a change of clothing at the entrance to the mine. The ruins of these can often be seen. Hand tools used in mining can be seen in museums at Buxton, Derby and Sheffield.

But, as mines went deeper, drainage became a problem and capital was needed to deal with it. Merchant partnerships were formed – sometimes specifically to drive a drainage channel (a *sough*) and sometimes to drain and operate the mine as well. In Shropshire these merchant partnerships were formed amongst local men during the eighteenth century – one John Lawrence was a leading investor. In Derbyshire, companies like the Gregory Mine Company and the London Lead Company had wealthy partners out of the county. In the nineteenth century the Lawrence empire was overturned by a group of rich Lancashire men.

As with coal and iron, the mineral rights in the lead mining areas were often held by the landed estates. The Dukes of Devonshire at Chatsworth, for example,

Below This engine house at Snailbeach mine was erected circa 1900. It contained a horizontal steam engine for processing the waste heaps.

Bottom right Wrought iron kibbles at Snailbeach. These were used to haul lead ore out of the mine.

PLACES TO VISIT

Buxton, Derby and Sheffield museums – miners' tools.

Ashover, Derbyshire – Gregory Mine, waste tips and chimney.

Snailbeach, Shropshire – abundant evidence of lead mining, adits, engine house, offices and kibbles.

owned large areas in Derbyshire and Staffordshire. And the Marquis of Bath owned the richest part of the Shropshire ore field, including the famous Snailbeach mine. The Marquis employed some of the leading mining engineers of the time and the Snailbeach Company made profits of £16,000 a year in the mid-nineteenth century. The most impressive remains of the Shropshire lead industry can be seen at Snailbeach where there are ruined engine houses, a mine office, a powder house, and *adit tails* and many other buildings.

After the passing of company legislation in the 1850s and 1860s, a number of limited liability companies were launched in Shropshire. But in the late 1860s, as the public confidence in Shropshire mines declined, there was a reversion back to smaller private companies. Ten years later new public company promotions began again – but lead prices started to fall and continued to do so until the end of the century. This made mining uneconomic in the county. In Derbyshire, where there had been 292 mines in the early nineteenth century, the large companies – such as Gregory and Mill Close Mine – ceased production. By the end of the century the only mining carried out in the county was conducted by small groups of men without capital, who lived a sort of hand-to-mouth existence. This is quite well documented by early photographs.

Drainage and production

Mine drainage problems were solved in several ways. In the seventeenth and eighteenth centuries, water-wheels operating pump rods were used. In Derbyshire wheels of up to fifty-two feet diameter were installed for this purpose. A Newcomen engine was installed at Yatestoop Mine before 1720 and, by 1730, two more had been added. Francis Thompson and Boulton and Watt installed engines towards the end of the century – early ones being used at Gregory Mine. Remains of an engine house can be seen at Tankerville, Shropshire.

The most spectacular method of drainage, however, was by a sough. This was a channel, often three or four miles long, constructed to carry water from the mines to a natural drainage outlet – such as a small stream. The exit, or tail, can sometimes be seen with neatly formed arches. Occasionally the initials of leading shareholders are inscribed on the key stone. These were great feats of engineering, and costly too. Hillcarr Sough, in Derbyshire, was nearly four miles long and had cost £50,000 by 1806. The first Derbyshire sough was driven by the Dutch engineer, Vermuyden.

When the ore had been raised in *kibbles* (cast iron buckets), it was crushed by stampers or edge runner stones, then washed in a device called a *jigging machine* or a *buddle*. Remains of ore crushing and washing plants can be seen in the Shropshire and Derbyshire orefields.

The final process was smelting. Many of the larger mining companies, like the Gregory Mine Company and the Snailbeach Company, owned smelt mills. Snailbeach smelt mill, built in 1784, still survives. Throughout most of the eighteenth and nineteenth centuries the *reverberatory furnace*, in which the fuel and ore did not come into direct contact, was used. This was introduced into Derbyshire by the London Lead Company in the 1730s. Remains of a later one can be seen at Moor Mine by Black Rocks, Cromford. In 1777,

PLACES TO VISIT

Tankerville, Shropshire – engine house.

Whatstandwell, Derbyshire – Meerbrook Sough outlet.

Cromford, Derbyshire – remains of lead smelting mill at Black Rocks.

underground *flues* were introduced to carry fumes from the mill to a chimney. Remains can be seen at Alport in Derbyshire, but physical remains of the lead smelting industry are more extensive in Yorkshire than in the Midlands.

Left Boulton's Soho Manufactory. It was here that parts of Boulton and Watt engines were made – as well as toys, buttons, buckles, sword hilts and many other objects.

Below The interior of Soho Foundry.

Copper

The veins of copper in north-east Staffordshire were extensively mined in the eighteenth and early nineteenth centuries. There were workings at Ribden, Calton Moor, Upper Elkstone, Mixon, Swinscoe and Ecton Hill. The richest ores, on Ecton Hill, lay within the Duke of Devonshire's estate. They were worked by the Duke until 1825, by which time they had ceased to be profitable. Groups of "adventurers" then attempted to find new veins and eleven separate enterprises are known to have existed between 1826 and 1890. These efforts, however, did not prove profitable.

Mining techniques at Ecton were advanced. Explosives were in use early, it was the deepest mine in Britain in the 1780s and boats were used underground. Drainage was less of a problem at Ecton than in the Derbyshire lead mines and an unusual method was adopted. The first drainage channel, Apes Tor Sough, had been cut before 1759. Later another channel was constructed, and the Apes Tor Sough was used to convey water *into* the mine to work a simple water engine – the function of the sough, therefore, had been reversed. In 1783, a water engine was built.

In 1772, a Swedish visitor to Ecton described the mines vividly. "Such a horrid gloom, such a rattling of waggons, such a noise of workmen boring rocks under your feet and such explosions in blasting and such a dreadful gulf to descend, present a scene of terror that few people not versed in mining care to pass through." Today, the most impressive remains of mining activity are the hummocks and spoil heaps, the adit tails and a Boulton and Watt engine house – now converted into a barn. The mine manager's house, the sales room and the offices have all been converted to dwellings, but a heap of rubble is all that remains of the school built by the Duke of Devonshire for the miners' children.

The Ecton mines reached the peak of prosperity in

PLACES TO VISIT

Broad Street, Birmingham – brasshouse.

Ecton, Staffordshire – engine house, mine manager's house, offices (now dwelling houses).

Opposite Birmingham Brasshouse, in Broad Street, was built in 1781 by a group of Birmingham manufacturers. The main building still survives and is the Weights and Measures Office.

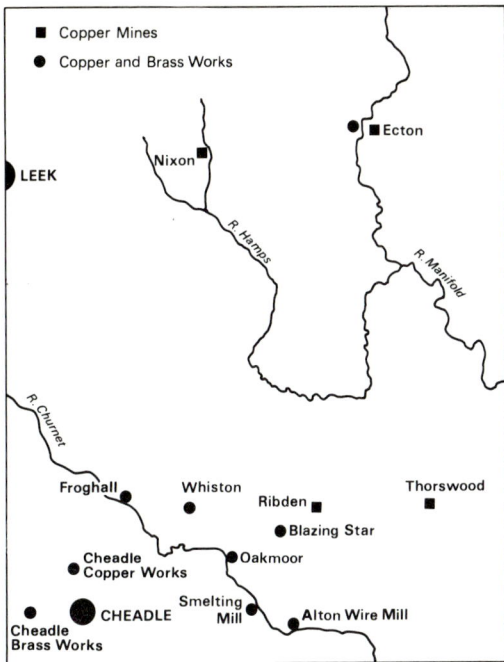

Above The copper mines, copper works and brass works in north Staffordshire.

the 1780s, when over 4,000 tons of ore were produced in a year. This figure was 12 per cent of the combined output of the Cornish mines, the major copper producing area. Considerable quantities of copper and brass were required in Birmingham and small metal manufacturers, such as Matthew Boulton, were keen to have as many sources of supply as possible. Boulton invested in Cornish mines and in a south Wales copper works, and he also looked towards Ecton and Cheadle for some supplies. But prices of manufactured copper and brass were rising. In 1781, Birmingham manufacturers formed a partnership to build a brasshouse in Broad Street, Birmingham, in an attempt to combat high prices. The principal building is now the Weights and Measures Office and is, without doubt, the finest industrial monument in central Birmingham. It is an attractive, two storey, classical building with *venetian window*, parapet and elegant doorway.

Metals – Nailmaking

The raw materials for many of the Black Country and Birmingham small metals trades included iron, but the end products were very varied. Noticeable local specializations had emerged by the end of the seventeenth century and these have persisted to the present day. There was a thriving trade in saddlers' ironmongery (associated with the leather industry) at Walsall and locks were made at Brewood, Wednesfield, Walsall, Wolverhampton and Willenhall. In the 1860s there were 450 locksmith firms in the Black Country employing 4,950 people – an average of eleven employees in each firm. Tin plate and japan ware were made in Wolverhampton and Bilston, and enamelling was a Bilston speciality. Edge tools, scythes and agricultural implements were made at the Lye near Dudley; tubes were made at Wednesbury, fire irons at Dudley, cast iron holloware at Birmingham and West Bromwich, and chains at Cradley Heath, Halesowen, Old Hill, Brierley Hill and Quarry Bank. The most widespread of all the industries in this region, however, was nail-making – although there was local specialization in different types of nails.

Nailmaking was to some extent the least skilled of the Black Country industries, for a child of nine could be employed at the hearth. It was also, from the mid-nineteenth century, the poorest paid occupation of the region. It was a domestic occupation, in which no division of labour was practiced. The nailer worked in a small forge or "shop" attached to, or near, his home. The average back yard nail shop was small, with a square unglazed window with bars and a low door. It was just large enough to house a hearth, an anvil, bellows, an *oliver* (foot operated hammer), a tool rack and the nailer. Many nailers' houses and workshops have been demolished in recent years, but two have been taken down and reconstructed. One is at Avon-

PLACES TO VISIT

Avoncroft Museum, Bromsgrove – nailers' workshop.

Dudley Museum – nailers' workshop.

Stour Valley – remains of water powered mills, many of which were originally slitting mills.

28

croft Museum of Buildings, the other at Dudley Museum.

Rod iron, purchased from a local slitting mill, was delivered to the nailer each week from the merchant manufacturer's or nail master's warehouse. The nailer, his wife and any of their children over nine forged the rod into nails. At the end of the week the nails were taken to the merchant and the nailer was paid. Sometimes the nailer was a semi-independent small master, who purchased small quantities of rod from the merchant and sold the product back to him. It has been estimated that 50,000 people were employed in the nail trade in 1830.

Below Two women nailmakers stand outside their shop. This photograph was taken about 1900.

The nail trade

As in other craft industries, some merchant manufacturers began to concentrate the production of nails by building hand nail shops containing several hearths alongside their warehouses. This saved the time spent in travelling to individual nailers and meant that the merchant could make sure that no petty thieving took place. On the other hand, it meant an outlay of capital in building the workshop.

By the beginning of the nineteenth century there were between forty and fifty merchant firms engaged in the nail trade. Government and dock contracts were important at this time. The East India Dock Company contract amounted to 110 tons a year before 1830 and, in 1820, the Admiralty contracted for about 640 tons of nails. There was also a considerable export trade to the U.S.A. and Canada. A merchant manufacturers' workshop containing eight hearths still exists in Mount Street, Halesowen. This has the normal unglazed windows and a chimney for each hearth. The interior is fitted up in much the same way as the individual nail shops and each hearth has its own oliver, *timber spring pole* and forging tools made by the nailers.

There was a great variety of hand-made nails for different purposes, but the highest quality were horse shoe nails. These not only required greater skill in the making, but also a better quality iron than other nails. They were made in and around Dudley. This branch of the nail trade remained prosperous until the mid-nineteenth century, while many other branches suffered. This was because attempts to mechanize the production of horse nails had failed, whereas the mechanization of other branches of the nail trade had succeeded and machine-made nails were ousting hand-made nails from the market.

Nailmaking was a hard way of life and this was reflected in the pastimes of the nailer. Bull baiting, dog-

fighting and cock-fighting were popularly practiced blood-sports long after they had become illegal. The hobbies of many Blackcountrymen of today – whippet and pigeon racing, fighting cock and bull terrier breeding – are direct descendants of these older sports.

Mechanization of the nail industry began on two fronts and there were considerable technical problems to be overcome on both. The cast nail was first patented in 1769, but the cut nail was more successful in the long run. Early experiments in the cut nail were made "at a heavy cost and serious loss," and the most successful cut nail invention eventually came from the U.S.A. The patent rights were sold to a London company, which opened the first steam-powered, cut nail factory – the Britannia Works – in a disused brewery in Birmingham in 1811. Although the factory-made nail had now captured the mass market, the hand nail trade struggled on in a much contracted form. It provided high quality nails for special purposes, and reverted in many instances to a part-time occupation for women – at least until the early twentieth century.

PLACES TO VISIT

Mount Street, Halesowen – large nail workshop.

Worcester County Museum – collection of nails.

Ironbridge Gorge Museum – an oliver.

Left A nailmaker's shop in the Black Country. This is still in use.

Chainmaking

There were many similarities between the Black Country nail and chain trades. Chainmaking, however, was more localized and was particularly concentrated in the Cradley Heath area. As in nailmaking the merchant sent our bar and rod iron to the chainmaker, who worked at the hearth in his workshop. The chainmaker's workshop was almost identical to the nailer's shop. Only some of the equipment differed. For example, the *tommy* was used as well as the oliver. And there were special tools for picking chain from the hearth and for shaping, hammering and cutting it. As in the nail trade many women were employed, and one or two still work on a part-time basis. And there were almost as many varieties of chain as there were of nails: harness chain, twisted chain, chain for harrowing and all kinds of anchor chain. In the 1830s some of the larger chainmakers also began to forge anchors and some of the heaviest anchors ever produced – including one for the *Titanic* – were produced in the Black Country.

In the late eighteenth and early nineteenth centuries, some merchant manufacturers began to build workshops containing several hearths near their warehouses. These sometimes had no more than six or eight hearths – like the shop in Hingley Street, Cradley Heath – but they could have as many as twenty. One of these larger shops has been reconstructed at the Avoncroft Museum of Buildings.

By the 1860s there were about 2,000 men and boys employed in chain factories, although there were still some 300 small domestic shops employing another 2,000 men, women and children. About 50,000 tons of chain and cable were produced every year and 10,000 tons of iron were used in the manufacture of small chain.

In 1969, there were two hand chain works left in the

PLACES TO VISIT

Hingley Street, Cradley –
chain shop.

Avoncroft Museum,
Bromsgrove – chain shop.

Noah Bloomer and Sons,
near Cradley.

Black Country. When Jones and Lloyds of Cradley Heath closed, Noah Bloomer and Sons was left as the sole survivor of a once thriving industry. There is still a limited demand for hand wrought chain and the traditional processes are carried out still at Noah Bloomer's. The chainworkers, for example, continue to work between 4.30 and 12 in the morning. The chain is hand forged, link by link, and the completed sections are hung over a hook near the hearth. When the chain is completed, it is tested by applying twice the pressure of the intended working load.

Below Chainmakers at work. Notice the tools that the men are using.

Needles and fish hooks

The needle and fish hook industry in the Midlands thrived in a small, clearly delimited, roughly triangular area between Bromsgrove and Alvechurch in the north, through to Feckenham, Alcester and Bidford-on-Avon in the south. Apart from the overlap with Bromsgrove's nail industry, itself a kind of outpost, the needle area was detached from the heart of the small metal trades. It was already firmly established by 1700 and became the dominant industry of the area, yet there is no satisfactory explanation for either its location or its growth. The main centres of the needle and fish hook industry – Redditch, Feckenham, and Studley – hardly gave the appearance of industrial towns. In 1843, a visitor wrote: "Here we get still more into the country, and marvel more that a seat of manufacture should be found there. We do not see waggons laden with manufactured goods, nor workmen hastening home to their meals; but we see women returning from Bromsgrove market, seated on rough little horses, with panniers on either side of them."

Water power was available from the rivers Alne and Arrow, tributaries of the Avon. But, on the first recorded occasion on which power was applied to a process of needle manufacture in this area, it was not water but horse power that was used. There was also a local supply of grindstones for sharpening needles, but neither of these features was exclusive to this area. One can only suppose that the rise of the needle industry along the borders of Worcestershire and Warwickshire was due to the initiative of a local person who made a success of his business, and that others were attracted by the possibility of being equally successful.

The merchant manufacturer was crucial in the organization of the needle and fish hook industry, for there was a minute division of labour. A needle had to pass through seventy hands before completion. Steel

PLACES TO VISIT

Redditch, Worcestershire – Forge Mill (needle mill).

Alcester, Warwickshire – Ragley Mill (needle mill).

34

wire was purchased from Birmingham and Sheffield and distributed to domestic outworkers, but the merchant manufacturer was the vital link in the chain. It was he who had to supervize the passing of the materials from one hand to another. In the early eighteenth century power was necessary during the processes of pointing and scouring and, from the 1730s, manufacturers began to convert water corn mills along the rivers Alne and Arrow. One of the first to be converted was Forge Mill, so named because of its former function. This mill has been preserved, through local initiative and effort, as a museum of the needle industry. It contains thirty-two scouring runner beds, drying barrels, ovens and stone crushing equipment.

Below This needlemaker's advertisement shows the two main purchasers of needles and fish hooks – the seamstress and the fisherman.

35

Needle factories

We know something of the activities of the merchant manufacturer in the needle industry through the records of the English family of Feckenham. Job English's business contacts ranged from Cumberland to Devon in the early eighteenth century. He had dealings with merchants in London, Bristol, Liverpool and Birmingham. He travelled on horseback, taking orders and leaving samples of needles to advertize his goods. Job was succeeded first by his son and then by his grandson, both named John. Under the younger John, needle manufacture was fully integrated at the steam driven Eagle Mill at Studley. Another branch of the family owned a needle factory in Queen Street, Redditch.

Below A small master's metal workshop in Birmingham.

PLACES TO VISIT

**Studley and Redditch –
Victorian needle factories.**

The first fully integrated needle factories were built in the early nineteenth century, but power was only applied to a few of the processes. The domestic producer, therefore, was not immediately displaced and for many years the factory and domestic systems of needle production operated side by side. In 1843, the *Penny Magazine* described a newly-built Redditch factory which consisted of a number of small courtyards: "The object of this arrangement seems to be to obtain as much light as possible in the workshops, since most of the departments of needle making require good light . . . The subdivisions of the factory correspond with those in the routine of manufacture . . . some of the (work)shops are occupied by men, others contain only females, and others again furnish employment chiefly for boys." About three thousand people were thought to be employed in the needle trade in Redditch – and there were between six thousand and seven thousand employed in the needle district as a whole. In the 1860s the wages of children ranged from 1/6d (7½p) to 5/– (25p) a week. Women earned 8/– (40p) to 15/– (75p), and men were paid 12/– (60p) to 40/– (£2) a week.

Fish hooks of all kinds were made in the area. They varied from the very small to the very large and came in an infinite variety of shapes. Artificial flies were made by women and girls. "In short," wrote an astute commentator in 1865, "wherever the finny tribes are found, there will be some of these products of Redditch manufacture found also."

Needle and fish hook manufacture is now concentrated in the towns of Redditch and Studley. Surgical needles are one of the special products of the much contracted industry today. But some of the old sharpening mills can be seen in ruin in the river valleys, and the small grindstones which lie around them are a clue to their former use.

Watch manufacture

Watch manufacture was an urban craft in the Midlands. It had first been introduced in Coventry and was well established by 1830. The trade was organized by a small number of master watchmakers. They performed some of the skilled operations themselves and delegated others to skilled journeymen who worked in their own homes. Errand boys were an important part of the system, for they carried the parts from one craftsman to another. There was a highly specialized division of labour, which meant that the watchmaking community was close-knit and interdependent. The specialized nature of watch manufacture ensured that, unlike the Coventry ribbon trade, there was no sudden influx of cheap labour which had to be dismissed when conditions worsened. Another difference between watch and ribbon manufacture in Coventry was that women were not employed in watchmaking, and the watchmaker earned as much by his labours as a whole weaving family.

Although by the 1850s there were watchmakers scattered all over Coventry, including some who lived in the ribbon weaving quarter of Hillfields, a distinct watchmaking quarter had evolved in Chapelfields. Most of the quarter still survives, although it is not inhabited by watchmakers any longer. The master watchmakers, unlike their counterparts in the ribbon trade, all lived within this area and this gave added stability to the trade as well as making for an integrated community.

Superficially, the houses of watchmakers were little different from those of ribbon weavers. They often had two rooms on each floor, but while the hand-loom ribbon weaver needed a whole floor for his looms the watchmaker needed only his bench against a window. The journeyman watchmaker's house in Chapelfields usually had two storeys at the front and three at the

PLACES TO VISIT
Chapelfields, Coventry – Allesley Old Road, Duke Street, Lord Street, Mount Street, Sir Thomas White's Street, Craven Street.
North Leys Lane, Ashbourne – clockmakers' workshop.

back. The workshop was generally the rear room on the first floor, which had long windows to give light. Whichever way the house faced, the workshop was always at the back. From the front, therefore, the watchmaker's house was just like any other suburban villa.

The master watchmakers lived at the north end of Chapelfields. They frequently had a row of workshops, for assembling the parts made by the journeymen watchmakers, projecting from the rear of their houses. Capacity could be increased by adding blocks to this projecting row and, today, the successive stages by which a business has been built up can be seen by the number of joins in the brickwork.

The masters' houses were somewhat grander than the small master ribbon weavers' houses in Hillfields. But foreign competition, and the slow transfer to larger units of production, meant decline for the Coventry watch trade and the Chapelfields workshops have been converted to other purposes.

Below A former master watchmaker's workshop in Chapelfields, Coventry. Notice the continuous row of windows on the first floor.

The gun trade

It was due to the efforts of Sir Richard Newdigate, one of the M.P.s for Warwickshire, that Birmingham gun manufacturers were given an opportunity to provide samples of their goods to His Majesty's Board of Ordnance. In 1692, they were given a contract to supply muskets. For much of the eighteenth century Britain was involved in war and these contracts were maintained. Birmingham manufacturers supplied more guns to the Board of Ordnance than London manufacturers. Between 1803 and 1816 they produced 1,827,899 arms for the Board while London manufacturers made only 845,477. If we add to this the number of gun materials made in Birmingham but assembled in London, as well as the sporting guns which were manufactured in peace time, we find that approximately five million guns were made in Birmingham between 1804 and 1815. This is more than the total output of the ten French government gun factories.

The Birmingham gun trade was based on a fine division of labour. For example, six different operations were performed by different workmen in the production of gun barrels alone. The production of gun barrels required power – for rolling, boring and grinding. The forges for this were located in the Deritend and Duddeston districts of Birmingham. By the mid-nineteenth century nearly all the London gun manufacturers purchased their gun barrels from Birmingham.

The safety of a gun depended upon the accuracy with which the barrel was bored. A gun was condemned as useless, for instance, if there was an error of only three-thousandths of an inch. Such workmanship was rewarded with high wages and it was possible to earn £5 to £6 a week in the trade in the mid-nineteenth century. To ensure that the finished barrels were flawless, the Board of Ordnance kept viewers in

Above A foot soldier in the mid-eighteenth century. The musket which he carries was probably supplied by Birmingham manufacturers.

Birmingham to inspect its own orders. In 1796, the Board agreed to provide a proof house at which the gun barrels made for the Government could be tested. This was built in Bagot Street and opened in 1797. At least one gun manufacturer had a private proof house, in which he proved his own and some other manufacturers' guns, and there were possibly others. But the Birmingham gun trade required a public proof house, as much for the preservation of its reputation as for the protection of its customers. This was built in 1813, and still stands, in Banbury Street. It is an attractive, two storey, dutch gabled, brick building with the Birmingham coat of arms in the centre and decorated drain pipes with the date 1813 cast at the top. The testing shops, with their louvred roofs to allow the escape of fumes after firing the barrels, the gunpowder store and other buildings lie to the rear of the Proof House by the canal.

PLACES TO VISIT

Banbury Street, Birmingham – Gun barrel proof house.

Below Grouse shooting. Birmingham manufacturers concentrated not only on the production of muskets – they also made sporting guns like those in the picture.

Gun merchants

The minute subdivision of labour in the gun trade necessitated a high degree of organization. This was the function of the merchant manufacturer who was responsible for putting out the work, at various stages in production, to the different specialists. This subdivision of labour still persists in the manufacture of high quality sporting guns.

In the early eighteenth century, a visitor to Birmingham went to "a Quaker's, to see the making of guns." The Quaker in question was probably one of the Galton family. Samuel Galton established his warehouse and workshops in Weaman Street and this may partly account for the rapid development of the Gun Quarter, for the smaller manufacturers tended to imitate the leader. It was also convenient to have their workshops close together and, by the end of the century, the gun trade was firmly located in the St. Mary's district.

Much of the Gun Quarter has been demolished in recent years, but a small amount remains in Princip Street and Bagot Street. Public houses like *The Gunmakers' Arms* are a reminder of the time when the Quarter was much more extensive. The block of workshops known as New Buildings, erected circa 1850, provides a good example of the organization of the gun trade. A worn notice board at the entrance provides places for about thirty names. The buildings are ranged around a courtyard and each shop contains a hearth, an anvil and bellows. Decorative tie irons mark the positions of workbenches by the windows in each shop.

Great fortunes were made in the gun trade. For example, in 1766 the total capital of Samuel Galton Junior's firm was £36,143. It was with these fortunes that the family bought a number of minor country houses in the west Midlands, including Warley Hall.

PLACES TO VISIT

St. Mary's district, Birmingham – Loveday Street, Princip Street, Price Street.

Smallheath, Birmingham – B.S.A. factory.

42

The gun trade was slow to adopt the factory system, chiefly because many of the operations could not be performed by powered machinery. Although this is now possible, some small workshops still produce barrels and locks in the Gun Quarter. Each gun was unique and, although guns with interchangeable parts had been made in the U.S.A. from at least the 1840s, no developments took place in England until the early 1850s. In 1854 a British Government arms factory, with a capacity of two thousand guns a week, was set up at Enfield. The first guns were produced four years later. Birmingham gun manufacturers were concerned at the competition of such a large scale factory and, forming themselves into a joint stock company, they built the Birmingham Small Arms Factory in Small-heath. The factory was planned in squares of forty feet. The main building, which still survives, was a fine Italianate brick structure designed in 1862 by T. W. Goodman. But even here, in contrast to Enfield, where all parts of the guns were made in the factory, "advantage has been taken of having the source of supply so near at hand to obtain certain parts in an unfinished stage from the manufacturers of the town."

Left A disguised gun factory in Birmingham's Gun Quarter. Notice the plain side elevation.

43

The toy trade

The word "toys" was used in the eighteenth and nineteenth centuries to describe all sorts of small goods – including jewellery, buttons, buckles, rings, seals, gilt chains, charms, snuff boxes, sword hilts, gun and dagger furniture and small articles of plate. Many different raw materials were required for such a variety of wares – such as steel, brass, copper, silver plate and enamels. In 1759 Birmingham manufacturers estimated that at least twenty thousand people were employed in the toy trade in Birmingham and neighbouring towns and that goods to the value of £600,000 a year were produced. Five-sixths of these were exported to Europe, Russia and America.

The merchant manufacturer was responsible for the purchase of raw materials and organization of the trade from his warehouse. He selected new designs and patterns, put work out to innumerable different craftsmen and was responsible for the sale of the finished product in a highly competitive market. Probably the greatest button and toy merchant manufacturer in the eighteenth century was John Taylor who, with Sampson Lloyd, founded Lloyds Bank. He claimed to be employing six hundred people in 1759 and he died, reputedly, with a fortune of £200,000.

There was a fine division of labour in the toy industry. For instance, seventy to eighty specific jobs were performed in the manufacture of a single button. Mobility between the workman class and the small master class was frequently possible. It was estimated in 1860 that nine out of every ten master jewellers working in Birmingham had originally been a workman. "All that is needed for a workman to start as a master," wrote a contemporary, "is a peculiarly shaped bench and a leather apron, one or two pounds worth of tools, and for material a few sovereigns, and some ounces of copper and zinc."

PLACES TO VISIT

Birmingham, first toy/ jewellery quarter – St. Paul's Square.

Birmingham, second toy/ jewellery quarter – Warstone Lane, Vyse Street, Hockley Street, Northampton Street, Frederick Street, Vittoria Street.

At first the workmen's and small masters' houses and workshops were spread throughout the centre and inner suburbs of Birmingham and, as modern clearance advances, these are now being swept away. By the 1790s, however, a distinct Toy Quarter was emerging and the jewellers and toy makers were beginning to build elegant houses along Newhall Street and in St. Paul's Square. Many well-known merchant manufacturers worshipped in St. Paul's Church and their gravestones and memorial tablets can be seen in the church and churchyard. By 1829 the toy trades were firmly located in the area north of St. Paul's Church and west of Great Hampton Street. But, by 1845, because of trade difficulties some of the 5,300 toymakers in the town had migrated to poorer houses east of Great Hampton Street. Finally the Jewellery Quarter moved to its present location – the streets immediately north of the first Quarter. The gold discoveries in California and Australia had led to a great expansion in the toy and jewellery trades and firms migrated to the larger houses in Vyse Street, Warstone Lane and Northampton Street. The larger houses were again used partly as living accommodation and partly as warehouse and workshop. Evidence of the boom in the jewellery trade can be seen in the variety of architectural details in some of the houses and small factories. They are in the style of Florentine palaces, Lombardy castles, medieval churches and Greek temples. Moulded and *encaustic tiles* can be seen in profusion. Parts of this Quarter have already been demolished, but no other town in Britain has such an attractive and well-preserved craft quarter as this.

Right A Birmingham toymaker's advertisement, showing the business's courtyard development behind two dwelling houses.

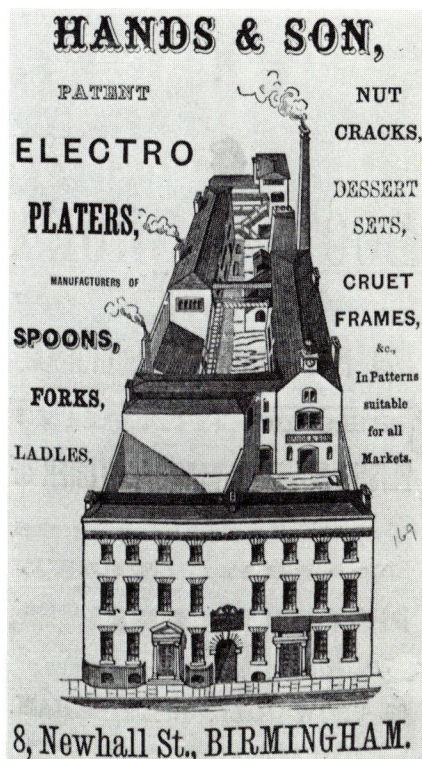

HANDS & SON,
PATENT
ELECTRO
PLATERS,
MANUFACTURERS OF
SPOONS,
FORKS,
LADLES,

NUT
CRACKS,
DESSERT
SETS,
CRUET
FRAMES,
&c.,
In Patterns
suitable
for all
Markets.

8, Newhall St., BIRMINGHAM.

45

Factory production

Even today the jewellery industry of Birmingham is partly domestic. The master jeweller may employ one or two workmen and his bench, apron, tools and materials have hardly changed since the 1860s.

The first factory had appeared in the jewellery trades, however, in the mid-eighteenth century – even before the cotton factories of Richard Arkwright. Matthew Boulton inherited a flourishing toy and button business from his father. He owned workshops in Snow Hill, Birmingham, and later on used New Hall (the ancestral home of the Colmore family) as a warehouse. In 1764 Boulton built a large and handsome factory in Handsworth, near Birmingham. Soho Manufactory, as it was called, consisted of a large, domed, rectangular block with a wing projecting at each end (see page 25). This building contained offices, some workshops and housing for employees in the wings. To the rear were courtyards, containing workshops and more dwellings. It was here that Matthew Boulton and his merchant partner, John Fothergill, aimed "to obtain a school of designers who would give to the products of the Soho Factory an artistic style and finish not obtainable elsewhere." Some of the pattern books of sword hilt, button and jewellery designs which were kept at the factory still survive.

Although Soho was a great showpiece in the west Midlands, Boulton's lead was not quickly followed. Few of the processes of toy, button or jewellery manufacture were mechanized, although ingenious hand operated machines were in use. For the majority of toy manufacturers, factory building was too costly and not necessarily advantageous. When other manufacturers, like Edward Thomason, did build factories they were on a smaller scale. None of the early toy, button, or jewellery factories survive today, but in the Birmingham Jewellery Quarter converted dwellings and

PLACES TO VISIT

Frederick Street, Birmingham – Argent Works.

Regent Street, Birmingham – Victoria Works.

Great Hampton Street, Birmingham – Pelican Works.

workshops are intermingled with small, post-1850 factories for electroplating, engraving and silver rolling. A fine example is the Argent Works, built in the Italian style.

The button trade differed from the rest of the toy trade in the high percentage of women employed. A well-known picture of the 1830s shows the interior of a button factory with rows and rows of women at the work benches.

The ornate Birmingham buttons display great skill and artistry, and there is a good display to be seen in Birmingham Museum and Art Gallery. There was also a considerable trade in pearl and bone buttons for the household market. There was a Birmingham saying, something of an exaggeration, that 5/– (25p) was sufficient capital on which to begin making pearl buttons. Certainly the small master jeweller seems to have been regarded as higher in the social scale than other small masters . . . "They reside in comfortable dwellings, their clothes are frequently good and do not portray the working man," wrote an observer in the nineteenth century.

Left A Victorian jewellery factory in Birmingham's Jewellery Quarter.

47

Textiles and Leather – Silk ribbon weaving

The finest ribbons in Europe were made at Lyons and St. Etienne in France, and Basle in Switzerland. Between 1768 and 1826, however, there was a prohibition on their import. But, as free trade policies began to be implemented, the prohibition was abolished in 1830 and a 25 per cent tariff was imposed instead. This meant that French and Swiss ribbons gained a large share of the upper class market, whilst ribbon manufacturers in Coventry supplied the middle and lower classes with fancy ribbons and Coventry, Derby, Leek and Congleton supplied the whole of England with plain ribbons.

The key figure in the early eighteenth century ribbon trade was the merchant manufacturer. In Derby, Leek and Congleton, where there were silk throwing (twisting) mills, some merchant manufacturers may have owned a mill as well as organized ribbon manufacture. Coventry merchant manufacturers, on the other hand, usually purchased thrown silk from London or Manchester merchants. Silk was a costly raw material and great capital was needed to enter the trade. At the end of the eighteenth century, therefore, the whole Coventry industry was controlled by about twelve established merchant manufacturers. Agents, called undertakers, collected silk from the merchant's warehouse and delivered it to weavers working at home. Some undertakers had small workshops of their own and became small masters on their own account. Little capital was necessary for weavers to become undertakers, but few undertakers could become merchant manufacturers.

Towards the end of the Napoleonic Wars, the London wholesalers who received the woven ribbons began to by-pass the established merchant manufacturers and deal directly with the undertakers. Many of these men became small masters almost overnight. The suppliers

PLACES TO VISIT

Blockley, Worcestershire – remains of small silk throwing mills, some converted to houses.

Hillfields, Coventry – Primrose Hill, King William Street, St. Peter Street, Albert Street, Wellington Street.

Leek, Staffordshire – silk weavers' cottages with long upper windows.

of silk in London gave five months credit, which allowed the new small masters to get the silk dyed, woven and sold to the wholesalers for cash within three months. The trade was now open to competition and, by the 1830s, the undertaker had disappeared in Coventry.

In the 1830s a new suburb was built on the east side of Coventry. Hillfields, as it was called, was rapidly inhabited by ribbon weavers and small masters. It became, in effect, a Ribbon Quarter. The weavers' houses were usually two or three storeys high and two rooms deep. In the two storey houses the workshop was frequently the back room on the first floor, so the typical weavers' windows along the width of the house are only to be seen at the back. In three storey houses, the workshop usually went the depth of the house and weavers' windows were installed at both the front and the back.

In the surrounding villages undertakers continued to organize the ribbon trade in the first half of the nineteenth century. Although these village weavers were essential in times of brisk trade they were the first, when trade slackened, to be laid off. "Last in, first out," recorded a contemporary, "they lived in almost complete subjection to the city which exploited them and kept them permanently on the margin of employment."

Left Eli Green's cottage factory is demolished. It was built between 1858 and 1859, in a triangle between Berry Street, Vernon Street and Brook Street in Hillfields, Coventry.

Fashion and factories

The ribbon industry was particularly vulnerable to changes in fashion. One unknown Coventry manufacturer kept a book of samples between 1805 and 1810, indicating in the margin which ribbons had met with most success. A spotted ribbon "sold well" in 1809, whilst a rust and yellow self patterned ribbon "did not sell very well." On November 2nd, 1810, "the Princess Amelia died . . . at 12 o'clock in the morning . . . a Deep Mourning for six weeks to begin on Sunday 11th November." This manufacturer was quick to bring out black ribbons, but others were less quick and within a few weeks it was noted: "Trade is very bad, no fancy ribbons selling. Several ribbon and silk manufacturers breaking and the mourning for Princess Amelia to continue till 11th February." This pattern book, together with other interesting exhibits including *Stevengraphs*, is in the Herbert Museum and Art Gallery at Coventry.

The original ribbon loom could only produce one ribbon at a time. By about 1770 the "Dutch engine loom" had been introduced, enabling the weaver to produce several plain ribbons at once. But fancy ribbons still had to be woven on the old loom. The Jacquard loom, invented in 1795, allowed several fancy ribbons to be made at a time and gradually ousted the engine loom. A Jacquard loom can be seen in Coventry Museum and it is occasionally worked.

It was easier to apply power to looms which produced plain ribbons and, for this reason, the power loom appeared in Derby earlier than in Coventry. The first steam powered factory was not built in Coventry until 1831 and the opposition of the weavers was so great that it was destroyed by fire within a few weeks.

By 1851 there were six large and six small power-driven factories in Coventry. But the weavers preferred the idea of taking the steam engine to their homes.

PLACES TO VISIT

Coventry Museum – exhibits relating to the silk trade, including Jacquard loom.

Cash's Lane, Coventry – Cash's factory.

Sometimes an engine was placed near two cottages and sometimes a long terrace was served by an engine. The first cottage factory was probably built in 1847 and, by 1859, there were three hundred cottage factories in Coventry. They had anything from two to six looms each. These are hard to identify on the ground, as much of Hillfields and the neighbouring district of Foleshill have been demolished. They were usually built around a square or triangle with the steam engine in the middle and remains of engine shafting can sometimes be seen inside.

In 1860, Britain signed the Cobden Treaty with France. One result of this was that French silks flooded the British market and the ribbon trade collapsed – only a short time after two great blocks of cottage factories had been built by model benevolent employers. One of these survives and the other has only recently been demolished. Eli Green, a ribbon manufacturer, built sixty-seven three storey houses in a triangle between Berry Street, Vernon Street and Brook Street in Hillfields, between 1858 and 1859. Two years earlier John and Joseph Cash, fancy ribbon makers, had decided to expand their business. One hundred houses were planned between the Coventry Canal and what is now Cash's Lane, although only forty-eight were actually built. With imposing mock Tudor windows and half-timbered gables, this cottage factory is an important monument to the Industrial Revolution in Coventry. Today, only Cash's (noted for name tapes) and a few smaller firms remain in a trade that once employed thousands.

Left The Cash brothers' cottage factory in Coventry.

51

Hosiery

In the eighteenth and nineteenth centuries the hosiery industry was widespread in the east Midlands. The first knitting frame had been invented in 1589. The inventor, the Rev. William Lee, was born and spent much of his life at Calverton, a village four miles north of Nottingham. This explains the original location of the industry.

The first knitting frame was a hand-operated machine with eight needles, or hooks, to the inch. William Lee taught some of his relatives to work the machine but applications for a patent were refused. The machine was finally taken to France – but it received as little encouragement as it had in England. From the mid-seventeenth century, however, use of the machine spread in the east Midlands – although London was the main centre of the hosiery industry. In the early eighteenth century cheaper goods, made from wool and worsted, were increasingly made on the knitting frame and the centre of the hosiery industry began to shift to the east Midlands, where there were supplies of yarn as well as skilled and cheaper labour. The east Midlands gained a further advantage when silk yarn was successfully produced by power-driven machinery in Derby, in the early eighteenth century. The number of frames employed in Derbyshire, Leicestershire and Nottinghamshire increased from about 3,500 in 1727 to over 25,000 in 1812 – out of a total of nearly 30,000 in the whole of Britain. The industry continued to increase its capacity during the first half of the nineteenth century, in spite of periods of depression and unrest.

The hosiery industry was organized on the domestic putting out system. The system survived until the middle of the nineteenth century – and later in some areas – and many buildings and machines have survived to illustrate a pre-factory system of production.

Below A young apprentice boy.

52

A merchant hosier purchased the raw materials and then distributed them personally, or through agents called *bag hosiers*, to the framework knitters who worked in their homes in the villages of Leicestershire and Nottinghamshire. By the end of the eighteenth century there were 199 merchant hosiers in Nottingham, 85 in Leicester, 23 in Hinckley and 13 in Derby. The Nottingham hosiers tended to concentrate on cotton, Leicester hosiers worked on worsted and Derby hosiers specialized in silk goods, but there was often a considerable overlap.

At the top end of the scale in the hosiery industry were such merchant princes as William Haynes, who started business in Nottingham in 1773. By 1812 he had (with his partners) nearly a thousand frames. Lower down the scale was John Coltman, the Leicester merchant hosier whose portrait was painted by Joseph Wright of Derby. Coltman and his partner, Gardiner, owned forty-three frames at the end of the eighteenth century. The merchant hosiers were recruited from wealthy backgrounds in the second half of the eighteenth century. Out of 146 apprentices bound to Leicester merchant hosiers between 1780 and 1800, for example, more than a third were sons of landed proprietors. The majority of top merchant hosiers were inventors, or purchasers of inventions, in the trade – such as Jedediah Strutt and Samuel Need, owners of the Derby Rib patent of 1758. Samuel Unwin, a merchant hosier of Sutton in Ashfield, won a Royal Society of Arts prize for an improvement to the stocking frame.

The hosiery factory

In the early eighteenth century knitting frames were usually placed in a living room of the operative's house. Plenty of light, however, was necessary and gradually long windows were incorporated into the buildings. Timber framed cottages which have been adapted for framework knitters can be seen at Sutton Bonnington and Shepshed. And at Crich, in Derbyshire, long windows were inserted under the eaves of a stone-built terrace house. With the expansion of the hosiery industry purpose-built dwelling houses, containing a workshop for frames, became common. These were usually built in terraces and, as rows of these cottages were built in rural areas, former agricultural villages were transformed into domestic industrial townships. Woodborough and Calverton, in Nottinghamshire, are good examples. Knitters' houses in villages to the east of Nottingham were usually two storeys high with ground floor workshops, while in the town of Nottingham and the villages to the west they were usually three storeys high with top floor workshops. Three storey cottages can also be seen at Shepshed in Leicestershire. These are substantial buildings with two, and often three, bedrooms. In Leicester, where urban building land was less scarce than in Nottingham, frameshops were more frequently built in gardens or yards behind the house.

As early as the 1720s a minority of merchant hosiers began to assemble knitting frames in larger workshops, employing poor apprentices to work them. In the 1760s larger houses were converted to factories and some good examples of these larger purpose-built workshops survive. A two storey, double-fronted house in Bulls Head Yard, Wigston, has a two storey workshop which could probably have accommodated some thirty frames. Other examples can be seen at Kegworth, Leicestershire, and Calverton, Nottinghamshire.

PLACES TO VISIT

Woodborough, Calverton and Shepshed – framework knitters' cottages.

Nottingham – Hine and Mundella's factory.

Leicester – Frisby Jarvis's factory.

Above The framework knitters' arms.

Until powered machinery was introduced, the widespread adoption of the factory system in the hosiery industry was not economic. Mark Isambard Brunel patented a rotary action machine in 1816, but it was not until the 1830s and 1840s that the application of power was seriously considered. The first power driven hosiery factory was opened at Loughborough, in 1839, by Paget. In 1845, a second factory was opened which contained steam powered, rotary machines. The machines were introduced in Leicester in the same year and, in 1851, Hine and Mundella built the first steam powered hosiery factory in Nottingham. This is the only early, steam powered, hosiery factory to survive. There are, however, some imposing late nineteenth century factories in Leicester. The finest of these is undoubtedly Frisby Jarvis's factory, in Northgate Street. The street elevation is four storeys high, with a centre section surmounted by a *pediment*. Elaborate cornices and brackets convey a Venetian impression which is not altogether inappropriate at this site near the canal.

Machine lace

There were many branches of the hosiery trade. A census of 1812 revealed forty-one in the fancy trade alone. But there was also an important off-shoot – the machine lace industry. Hand made lace was an important domestic industry in Northamptonshire, where it remained until the first few decades of the nineteenth century. But the adaptation of the stocking frame to lace manufacture in the late eighteenth century created an entirely new industry. This was concentrated in Nottingham. Thus the machine lace industry grew up in a town whose inhabitants were relatively unfamiliar with the product they were attempting to copy by machine.

Framework knitters, like Birmingham button and buckle makers in the eighteenth century, were constantly attempting to produce new designs. Some ideas were patented, but many more were the fruits of the inventive skills of anonymous artisans. In the 1760s a means of producing a crude net on the stocking frame was discovered, but the lace industry made little progress until the invention of the *point net machine* in the 1770s. Large quantities of cheap net and lace fabrics were soon being produced and, by 1810, there were between 1,500 and 1,800 point net machines in Nottingham. These gave employment to 15,000 townsfolk, besides those who embroidered the net by hand in neighbouring villages. The lace machine was intricate, requiring considerably more skill to operate than the stocking frame. Consequently, wages were higher – 20/– (£1) to 40/– (£2) per week was usual at the end of the eighteenth century.

A crucial development in the machine lace industry was the invention, by John Heathcoat, of the bobbin net machine. This was patented in 1808 and improved in the following year. It could produce a fabric closely

PLACES TO VISIT

Newarke Houses Museum, Leicester – hosiery machinery.

Nottingham Castle Museum – lace and hosiery machinery.

resembling hand made lace. Another major invention was Leaver's bobbin and carriage machine, in 1813. This allowed more intricate patterns to be made. Models of both these machines can be seen in the Castle Museum, Nottingham. When Heathcoat's patent expired, in 1823, the machine lace industry expanded rapidly. The number of bobbin net machines increased from one thousand in 1820 to five thousand in 1833, with a high concentration in and around Nottingham and a smaller concentration in Loughborough. The Jacquard principle was applied to Leaver's machine in 1841. This enabled fancy lace to be made according to a predetermined pattern. Further expansion of the industry took place during the last two decades of the nineteenth century, when Victorian fashion demanded quantities of lace for clothing and furnishings.

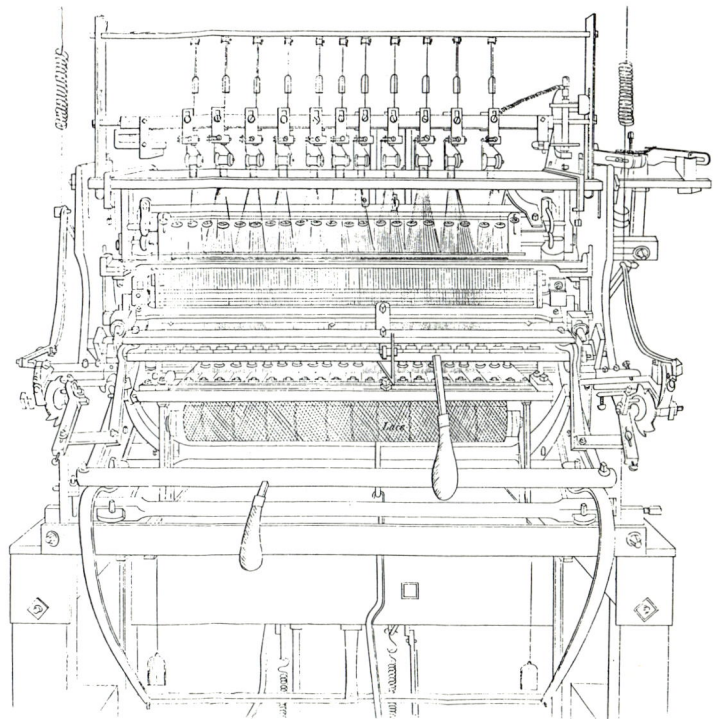

Right John Brown's bobbin net machine.

The lace industry

The organization of the domestic industry was similar to that of hosiery. Lace machines, like stocking frames, were hand operated and kept in the upper rooms of dwellings. During the 1820s terrace rows with top floor workshops, similar to those erected for hosiery workers, were built. Most of these were in the old villages – such as Hyson Green, New Radford and New Basford – which were gradually absorbed as suburbs of Nottingham. A typical domestic lacemaker's house was three storeys high, with an attic. There were generally two rooms on each floor and a small back yard containing a wash house. There were long windows at both back and front to light the workshop.

Unlike the hosiery industry, the lace industry was not solely domestic in organization in the 1820s. Larger workshop factories existed for hand machines and power had already been applied in some factories. Machines were larger and more costly than knitting frames and there was, perhaps, less dislike of the factory system in this new and prosperous trade. John Heathcoat's factory at Loughborough contained fifty-five machines by 1816. Steam power was in use at Boden and Morley's factory at Castlefields, Derby, which has been recently demolished. In 1843 there were approximately thirty powered lace factories and forty hand machine lace factories in England. The majority of these were in the east Midlands, but few survive. There is much more evidence today of the second lace boom, in the 1870s. Rapid expansion of the industry took place in Beeston, Chilwell, Sandacre, Stapleford and particularly Long Eaton. *Flatted factories*, which provided "room and power" to a number of separate firms, are a feature of this period. Some of these were built by larger established firms, some were built by lace machine makers, and others were constructed by people unconnected with the industry as a speculation.

PLACES TO VISIT

Nottingham Lace Market.

Nottingham, New Basford and Hyson Green – lace workshops in cottages.

Beeston, Nottinghamshire – Anglo Scotian Mills.

These buildings can be seen in the southern part of Nottingham, in Radford and in Basford. One of the largest is in Leopold Street, Long Eaton. It is seven hundred feet long. Most of these late Victorian lace factories have little architectural detailing. One exception, however, is Anglo Scotian Mills, Beeston, which has a crenellated parapet, turrets and gothic windows. Crenellated turrets were also a feature of a smaller mill at Chilwell, which was possibly under the same ownership.

By the 1820s, the wealthier Nottingham lace manufacturers lived in fine Georgian town houses in the central part of the town – near St. Mary's Church, along Houndsgate and east of the castle. Like the Birmingham toy manufacturers they probably used a room as office and warehouse. But, gradually, the houses and gardens in Broadway, Stoney Street and St. Mary's Gate were cleared away and replaced by the offices and warehouses of the successful lace manufacturers and merchants. The area became known as the Lace Market. The architecture is impressive and elaborate monuments were erected in memory of the successful lace trade. The warehouses are tall brick buildings and most of them contain large windows on the top floor. It was here that mending and hand finishing was carried out. The most elegant building is Thomas Adam's warehouse, built in the early 1850s in the shape of an E. The building is very elaborate, and there was a small chapel in which the employees worshipped each day.

Left Thomas Adam's warehouse in Nottingham's Lace Market. The building is in the shape of an E and is very elaborate both inside and outside.

Carpet manufacture

Carpet manufacture was well established in Kidderminster by the early eighteenth century. It had grown from the foundations of an even older woollen industry. The mechanization that affected the woollen and worsted industries at the end of the eighteenth century, however, had relatively little impact on the carpet industry. It meant only that yarn, which carpet manufacturers did not spin, could be obtained more readily. There were many problems to be overcome in carpet weaving before the power loom could be adopted with any degree of success, and it was not until after 1850 that the Kidderminster and Stourport carpet industry was mechanized.

These two towns ranked first amongst the carpet manufacturing areas of Britain and, by the mid-nineteenth century, produced more than a fifth of the total national output. It was estimated that there were some 2,300 carpet looms in Worcestershire out of a total of some 6,700 in the country. Kidderminster and Stourport's lead had been built on the production of high quality Brussels and Wilton carpets. The cheaper Kidderminster carpet, for which the town was formerly the chief producer, had been almost abandoned by this time. But a cheap imitation of the Brussels carpet was invented in the mid-nineteenth century, by the Halifax firm of Crossley. At the same time, they began to experiment seriously with power looms and acquired the patent rights for several of these. Crossleys, instead of attempting to monopolize the power loom production of carpets, readily sold licences to other firms. They also reduced their own carpet prices, in an attempt to bring carpets to those who were less well off and so to increase their sales. Faced with this situation, the Kidderminster manufacturer had to adopt power looms or face extinction.

At the beginning of the nineteenth century, carpet

PLACES TO VISIT

Kidderminster, Worcestershire – late nineteenth century carpet factories.

manufacturers had begun to build two and three storey workshop factories for hand looms. This was to enable them to supervize work more closely. But, since the Brussels power loom took up twice as much space as the Brussels hand loom, these factories were generally too small to be converted into power loom factories. In the early 1850s there were seventy-four hand loom factories in Kidderminster. Fifty of these contained twenty looms or less, and only three had more than sixty looms. A few of these smaller hand loom factories can still be seen.

The new power loom weaving factories were spacious, single storey buildings with the roof supported on iron pillars. In the early 1850s a factory capable of holding twenty power looms, with warehousing and offices, cost £3,000. The steam engine cost £500 and the looms £1,200 – a total of £4,700. This was a relatively low price to pay for mechanization and capital was forthcoming, both from within the carpet trade and from other sources. By 1856 the transfer to the power loom factory system was almost complete. By the early 1860s the mechanized Kidderminster carpet industry had a major share of the Brussels carpet trade and manufactured one quarter of the total British carpet production. Today these carpet mills still dominate the town.

Left Apprentice weavers (Hogarth). Hours were long and the work tedious, so overseers were needed to stop idling.

Footwear

The manufacture of boots and shoes, for more than a purely local market, was an important industry in Stafford, Northampton, Kettering and Leicester in the early eighteenth century. It was organized on the putting out system. Shoe uppers were cut out at a central workshop and were then sent out to hand sewers and finishers, who worked in their own houses or in a workshop at the bottom of their gardens. These "shops" can still be seen in Northamptonshire villages. A domestic outworker produced about seven pairs of shoes a week in the early nineteenth century. But, as in other industries, the larger merchant manufacturer

Below An early shoemaker works by hand in his shop.

62

had begun to collect domestic outworkers into a central workshop by the 1770s. William Horton of Stafford was one such man. He seems to have been the first to establish a large workshop in the town and employed about a thousand workers (some working in their own homes) towards the end of the eighteenth century. Horton not only supplied London merchants with shoes, he also did considerable trade with north Germany and the Baltic. Before the outbreak of the Napoleonic Wars he had an estimated annual output of £75,000 worth of shoes. By 1787 there were four more important shoe manufacturers in Stafford and Stone was also becoming a centre for shoe production.

The emergence of Kettering as an industrial town owes much to the enterprise of a single boot and shoe firm, Gotch and Sons. When Thomas Gotch moved to Kettering in the 1770s most of the non-agricultural workers were employed in textile manufacture. The foundation of Gotch's success lay in his ability to secure Government contracts for army and navy boots. England was at war with America when he started his business, and shortly afterwards war broke out with France. The orders he undertook were so large that he had to subcontract a great deal. This delegation was to be an important factor in the survival of the Kettering shoe trade.

Shoemakers' wages in the early nineteenth century were higher in Stafford than in Northampton – 1/6d. (7½p) rather than 1/4d. (7p) – and Stafford began to lose orders to Northampton. One leather dealer blamed high food prices for the loss of orders in Stafford. "Provisions being so high," he wrote, "the poor were forced to go nearly barefoot to supply their stomachs before their feet." During the same period, however, the Gotch enterprise in Kettering was flourishing on Government contracts. Between May and July 1813, the firm supplied 64,000 pairs of boots.

Mechanization of the shoe industry

In 1812 Mark Isambard Brunel developed a means of rivetting the shoe upper and sole together by machinery in his Battersea factory. Mechanization did not take place elsewhere, however, until the mid-nineteenth century. In the 1850s the first sewing machine arrived from America and, with slight modification, they could be used for closing the uppers of shoes. By 1859, North-ampton manufacturers announced that they could no longer delay the introduction of "machine sewn tops." Edwin Bostock was the first Stafford manufacturer to introduce the closing machine, but hand craftsmen were alarmed and attempted to delay the introduction of machinery in the town. The complete mechanization of the shoe industry, however, required a large number of different machines and it was almost impossible for a firm to purchase them all. So a system of leases and royalties was evolved, which continues to the present day.

By the late nineteenth century the typical shoe factory was a logically planned unit. Steam power was used to drive the machines and the operations which required the most daylight and the lightest machines were performed on the top floor of the building. Lasting and attaching machinery was worked on the floor beneath and at ground level, sometimes half below ground, were housed the leather store and the heavy cutting out machines. This system can be seen in many of the surviving Northampton shoe factories. But, by comparison with other industries, hand craftsmanship is still an important element in many branches of the shoe industry and in one or two specialized areas (such as high quality sports shoes) work is still done in small domestic workshops. One rugby boot maker still works with his three employees in a former carpenter's shop, behind his home in Towcester.

PLACES TO VISIT

Northampton, Kettering and Leicester – many late nineteenth century shoe factories.

64

In 1857, at the beginning of the age of machinery, Gotch's boot and shoe firm collapsed. But this was not the great disaster for Kettering that some people had feared, for a number of small masters were able to fill the gap left by this failure. By the 1860s at least twelve firms had emerged and were able to consolidate, through the gradual adoption of machinery, Kettering's staple industry.

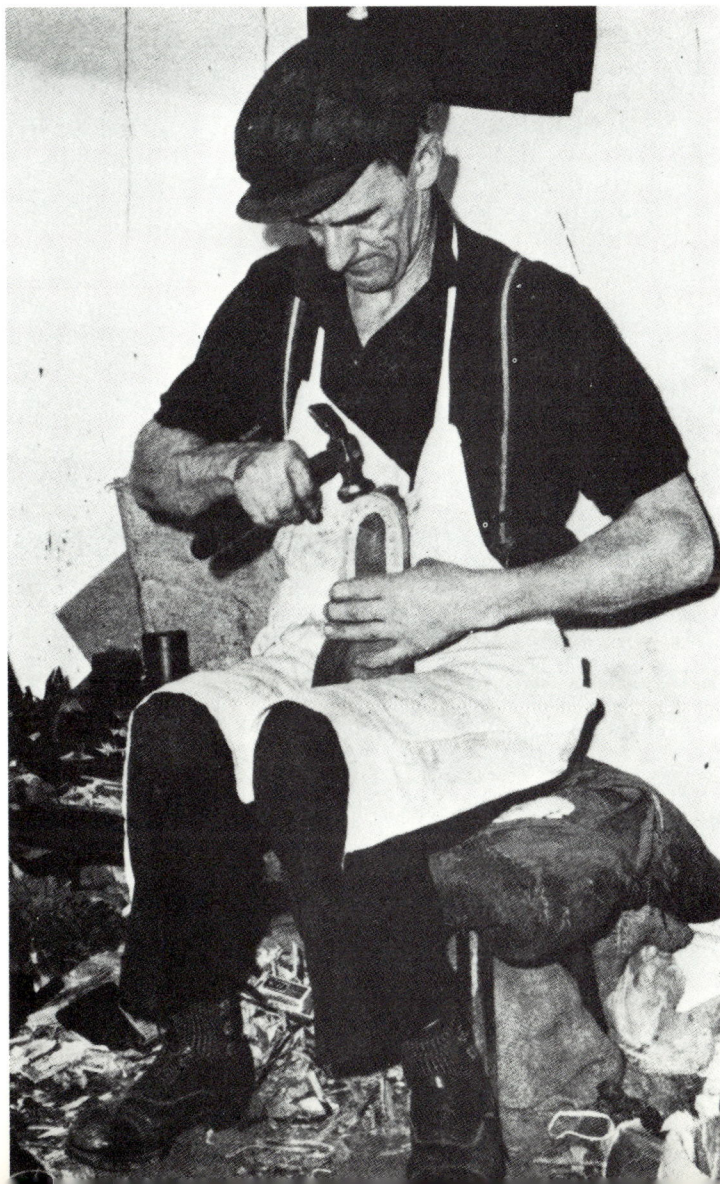

Left Hand craftmanship is still an important element in many branches of the shoe industry. This photograph was taken at Yorke's shoe factory, at Long Buckby, in 1969.

Mills and Factories – Silk

The origins of the modern factory can be traced back to the first British silk mill. This was built for Thomas Cotchett in Derby, in 1702, by the engineer George Sorocold. It was a water powered factory – 62 feet long, 28 feet 5 inches wide and 3 storeys high. More well known than Cotchett's mill, however, is the one that was built alongside it by Thomas Lombe, a wealthy London silk merchant. In 1718 Lombe obtained a patent which entitled him to the sole use of the throwing machinery for fourteen years and, by 1721, his mill was completed. Sorocold was again the engineer, but Lombe's factory was much more ambitious than Cotchett's. The throwing mill – called the Italian Works – was 110 feet long, 39 feet wide and 5 storeys high. The flat roof was hidden by a battlemented parapet. Nearby was a *doublers'* shop which could hold 306 machines. A fine pair of wrought iron gates, made by Robert Bakewell, were erected by the entrance to the works. Both Lombe's and Cotchett's mills have now been demolished, but the gates have been re-erected outside Derby Borough Library.

It is unlikely that Lombe's mill ever reached capacity production. But, when one considers his outlay of capital, it is remarkable that he managed to remain in business at all. When his patent expired, in 1732, a number of other silk mills were erected. There were twelve in Derby by 1789 and others were built at Chesterfield and Nottingham. A cotton mill at Maythorne, near Southwell (Nottinghamshire), was converted to silk manufacture in the late eighteenth century. This was part of a self-contained industrial hamlet, with industrial housing and a mulberry tree – a symbol of the trade. An interesting west Midlands outpost of silk throwing developed at Blockley in Worcestershire, where there were five or six small mills along the stream. Other mills were built in Maccles-

PLACES TO VISIT

Derby – gates from Lombe's mill outside the central library.

Beeston, Nottinghamshire – silk mill.

Above Silk doublers at work in the Derby Silk mill, in the 1840s.

66

field and Congleton.

The largest silk mill in the Midlands in the mid-nineteenth century was at Beeston. It was built in 1826, destroyed by fire in the Reform Bill riots, and almost immediately rebuilt. The 1860 treaty with France exposed Britain's silk industry to French competition, which few firms could withstand. Many Midlands mills were forced to close, some were converted to other uses and others were demolished.

Below The first factories in Derby. Thomas Cotchett's mill is on the right and Lombe's mill is in the centre.

Cotton

The demand for cotton yarn increased in the east Midlands during the eighteenth century, as hosiers began to use it as a cheaper alternative to worsted. In Lancashire, cotton was required for the manufacture of *fustian* cloth and by the middle of the century demand in both the Midlands and Lancashire had begun to outstrip the supply. Around 1764, however, James Hargreaves invented the spinning jenny. This, although it was not a powered machine, increased yarn production because of the larger number of *spindles*. While perfecting his machine, Hargreaves was persecuted during the "Jenny Riots" in Blackburn. Shortly afterwards he moved to Nottingham, where he went into partnership with Thomas James and built a jenny workshop. Hargreaves's machine was smaller than the stocking frame. This meant that, instead of hastening the development of the factory system, it enabled spinning to remain a cottage industry in the Midlands. Jenny workshops were more common in the north Midlands than around Nottingham and houses, cottages, barns and outhouses were converted. An example of a larger jenny workshop can be seen at Winster in Derbyshire. In 1795 this contained carding machines driven by a small atmospheric steam engine, spinning jennies and looms. One of the original partners was a grocer and the building survives today as the village store. Many owners of smaller workshops in north Derbyshire and Staffordshire combined cotton spinning with farming. Some of the more successful were able to graduate to larger enterprises by adopting Arkwright's water frame and migrating to a site by a stream. Edale Mill, for example, was built by a farmer cotton spinner in the 1790s. It is an attractive mill in a remote situation, but cotton was spun there as late as 1933. It is now being converted into flats – an original way in which to preserve an industrial monument.

A crucial stage in the development of the cotton industry was the introduction of roller spinning by Richard Arkwright. Whether Arkwright invented the machine or not, and he probably didn't, his genius for organizing men and machines is beyond dispute. Arkwright was a barber by trade, and it was as a traveller in search of hair for wigs that he first entered the Midlands. In 1769, the year in which he took out his first patent, he moved to Nottingham. With the backing of a local bank he built a mill which was driven by nine horses and contained a thousand spindles. In 1771, in partnership with two local merchant hosiers – Samuel Need and Jedediah Strutt – he built his first water powered spinning mill at Cromford. This was not the first water driven, cotton spinning mill. The first had already been built in Northampton and was equipped with spinning machines designed by Wyatt and Paul. That venture, however, was a failure and the successful application of water power to spinning dates from the first mill at Cromford. Arkwright was clearly an able mechanic and a superb businessman.

Nothing of Arkwright's mill at Nottingham survives today, but part of the shell of the first mill at Cromford still stands. The factory site was developed over a period of about twenty years and a number of the later mill and warehouse buildings also remain. Above all, the township of Cromford is a monument to Arkwright – he built many of the houses, an inn and a market place for his employees, and his descendents built a fine school.

Top left An old print of Jedediah Strutt's mills at Belper, in Derbyshire.
Left Edale Mill, in Derbyshire, was a remote cotton mill built by a farmer cotton spinner in the 1790s.

Arkwright's contribution

Richard Arkwright's contribution to the industrial development of the Midlands was enormous. With his move to Nottingham the Midlands, for a while, took the lead in the English cotton industry. Arkwright himself built mills in partnership with other manufacturers at Cressbrook (1783), Bakewell (1782), Masson (1784), and possibly Ashbourne in Derbyshire (circa 1781), and Rocester in Staffordshire (1782). He also granted licences to build many others. Strutt and his son, for example, had built five mills by the end of the eighteenth century at Belper, Milford and Derby. Gardom and Pares developed a fine site at Calver. The industry also developed away from the main Midlands area at Burton-on-Trent, Fazeley and Warwick, where the Smart family built a mill. Arkwright's mills were about 70 feet long and 30 feet wide, and initially cost about £2,000 (including machinery). When Arkwright wished to expand his works he added, as he did at Cromford, to the length of the original building. The Evans family did the same at Darley Abbey. The Peel family, on the other hand, preferred to increase their production by building a new mill rather than expanding the old one.

By the time of Arkwright's death another spinning machine, the mule, had been invented. This was hand operated at first, but water power was applied from the 1790s. Crompton's mule was a large machine with a moving carriage, which meant that it could not be installed in the Arkwright mills. Since they had already invested heavily in these mills, the water frame spinners of the Midlands did not adopt the mule. It was at this point that Lancashire gained control of the cotton industry although, for a while, water frame spinners managed to compete by concentrating on the spinning of coarser yarns than the mule produced. It was only a matter of time before the Midlands cotton spinning

Above Cressbrook Mill, in Derbyshire, is one of the most attractive small cotton mills. An earlier Arkwright mill adjoins it.

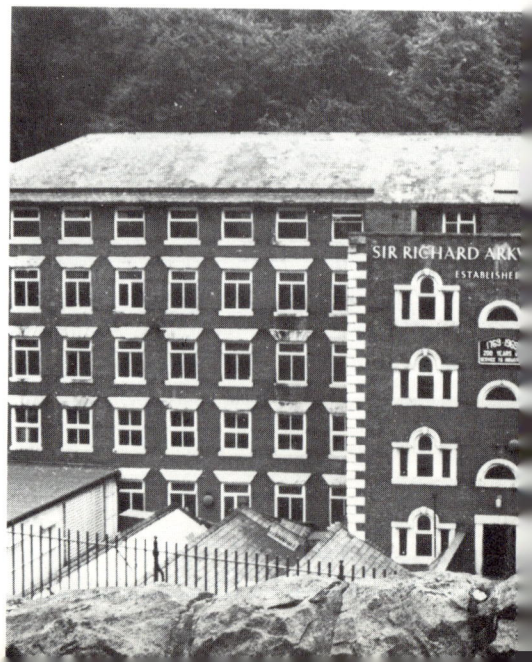

industry began to contract. Nevertheless, spinning is still carried out at several eighteenth century sites under the control of national companies. Masson Mill, Rocester Mill, Darley Abbey and Belper are still spinning mills and Masson and Rocester show a fine appreciation of classical architecture. Belper North Mill (1802–3) is one of the earliest fireproof mills in Britain and is in a fine state of repair. The Midlands is rich in remains of the water power era of the cotton industry.

When the early cotton spinners moved into the heart of Derbyshire and Staffordshire in search of water power, they were often far from a source of labour. In such cases they were forced, like the Shropshire ironmasters, to build houses to attract workers. Some manufacturers employed poor apprentices and an apprentice house with gothic overtones survives today at Cressbrook Mill. But there was greater stability in employing families and the villages of Cromford, Darley Abbey, Fazeley, Belper and Milford were virtually created by the cotton industry.

Below Masson Mill, near Cromford, was built by Richard Arkwright in 1769. Notice the similarities between this mill and Rocester Cotton Mill in Staffordshire (*below right*).

Worsted

From the mid-eighteenth century some regional specialization took place within the hosiery industry. The Leicester area, for example, concentrated on worsted. Some merchant hosiers in the area combined wool combing and spinning with their hosiery business, while others maintained close contact with the wool-combers. But the great growth of the hosiery industry, as well as the Kidderminster carpet trade, led to a shortage of yarn and supplies had often to be obtained from as far away as Bristol. With the inventions of Hargreaves, Arkwright and Crompton, hosiers saw possibilities for easing the situation. All three machines had been designed for and first applied to the cotton industry, but the spinning jenny was rapidly adapted to wool spinning. It was soon apparent that it was unsuitable for the longer staple worsted, however, and an answer was sought in the modification of Arkwright's water frame. The earliest attempt was made by a Nottingham man who had assisted Arkwright in his experiments, but the first success was achieved by John Coltman of Leicester. The machine was improved by one of Coltman's employees, Joseph Brookhouse. The Corporation of Leicester, however, refused to allow them to set up in business as worsted spinners within a fifty mile radius of the town.

Coltman moved to Bromsgrove, where he went into partnership with his nephew who owned a small cotton spinning mill. But the partnership did not last. Brookhouse moved to Warwick where he went into partnership with members of a well-known local family, the Parkes. They built a mill of typical Arkwright proportions at Saltisford, just off the Birmingham road, and housing in Parkes and Brookhouse streets. This mill still exists, but most of the housing has been demolished. The firm prospered by selling yarn to Kidderminster carpet manufacturers and Leicester hosiers. Other mills

PLACES TO VISIT

Saltisford and Warwick – worsted mills.

72

were built at Wolverhampton and Bedworth in the west Midlands and at Cuckney, Retford, and Arnold near Nottingham. A worsted enterprise at Louth deserves mention, for it strictly belongs to the Midlands worsted area. This mill was supported "by subscription of the Gentry, Proprietors and occupiers of lands," including Sir Joseph Banks whose family seat was nearby.

Spinning by power did not return to Leicester until 1818 when Thomas Fielding, who had been Parkes's and Brookhouse's Leicester agent, built his own factory in 1818. This brought about the collapse of the Warwick firm. Steam power was installed in Fielding's mill in 1822 and by the 1830s Leicester had taken the lead in power worsted spinning.

Below The worsted mill built by Parkes, Brookhouse and Crompton at Warwick.

Flax

The establishment of a large, mechanized, flax spinning industry in a single town in the Midlands is due to the energies and abilities of two Shrewsbury merchants – Thomas and Benjamin Benyon. In 1780 they began putting out yarn to local weavers and from 1791 were important customers of John Marshall, the Leeds flax spinner. When, in 1793, Marshall sought new partners for his Leeds business the Benyon brothers joined him with £9,000. As soon as Marshall's building programme had been completed in Leeds, the Benyons pressed for the establishment of a factory in Shrewsbury. Marshall opposed the scheme but could not prevent it.

In 1796 a site was purchased in Castle Foregate, Shrewsbury, and a twenty horse power Boulton and Watt engine was ordered. Flax spinning by power, another adaptation of Arkwright's principle of spinning by rollers, was first patented by Kendrew of Darlington. There were still, however, many problems to be overcome. The mill that the Benyons built was not only the first large factory in Shrewsbury and the largest single flax factory in the country, it was also the first iron framed building in the world. This unique factory is

PLACES TO VISIT

Shrewsbury – Castle Foregate Mill, housing and apprentice housing.

Left Castle Foregate Flax Mill at Shrewsbury. This was the first iron framed building in the world.

now a maltings, but the only modification to the original structure is the bricking-up of some of the windows. The mill is five storeys high and two hundred feet long. The roof slates are placed over the upper ceiling's brick arches, which give it a zig-zag outline. In 1798–99, a cross building was added and a forty horse-power engine, made by the Leeds engineers Fenton, Murray and Wood, provided the power. Marshall took over Castle Foregate Mill which was valued, when the partnership broke up in 1804, at £64,000. The Benyons took their share and built new mills in Leeds and Shrewsbury.

The development of the Castle Foregate mill continued. Gas lighting, a flax warehouse, a dyehouse and an apprentice house were built between 1808 and 1811, and workers' housing was provided on a large scale. Both the large Shrewsbury flax mills, however, finally failed – mainly because the second generation of owners concentrated their interests in Leeds. The Benyon mill at the Canal Terminus has been demolished but Marshall's mill still stands as an austere industrial monument.

Below left Mid-nineteenth century decorative iron work on the roof of Castle Foregate Mill.
Below The zig-zag roof at Castle Foregate.

Pottery

Few regions can boast such a list of internationally known names as Wedgwood, Spode, Copeland, Minton, Royal Worcester and Royal Crown Derby. These and many others can trace their ancestry back to the late eighteenth and early nineteenth centuries, when pottery manufacture developed from being a widespread craft industry to a scientifically based factory system of production. This does not mean, however, that the craft pottery was put out of business when larger pottery factories were built. The large and small firms existed side by side into the twentieth century, although the smaller firms declined in numbers.

The Potteries emerged as an identifiable manufacturing area before the coming of the factory system. There were already forty-seven pot works in the area by 1715, in which production was carried out by the master potter and his family. None of these potteries employed more than six workers and none had an output of more than £6 worth of goods a week. A map of Burslem drawn in 1750 shows that the area was still very rural, but the number of potworks was increasing. These small units consisted of the master's house, with a workshop and a kiln in the back yard. As more work space was required, additional shops were built around the outside of the yard. Thus emerged the courtyard plan which is so typical of potteries large and small. In 1769 Arthur Young visited the Potteries and estimated that there were three hundred firms in business employing on average twenty persons per works. In 1835 there were approximately 130 factories employing 20,100 workers and the number of employees had probably risen to about 25,000 by 1850.

Many eighteenth to mid-nineteenth century Staffordshire potters were not only potters but also owners of land. Some, like Josiah Spode, lived in large houses. And some, like Wedgwood, were shareholders in canals

PLACES TO VISIT

Etruria, Staffordshire – housing and chapel.

Cheddleton, Staffordshire – flint mill and museum.

Trent and Mersey Canal, promoted by Josiah Wedgwood.

Above An early drawing of Josiah Wedgwood's factory at Etruria. *Below* William Adam's classical Greengates Pottery, built in 1770.

and other companies.

Power requirements in the pottery industry were small. Most of the operations were done by hand and required great skill. One of the processes – flint crushing – had been mechanized in the early eighteenth century. Crushed int was added to the clay or used as a glaze in biscuit ware. The north Staffordshire Potteries were poorly supplied with water power. The most suitable stream, the Churnet, was several miles away to the east. For this reason few of the smaller potters carried out flint crushing, but bought what they needed from the larger firms or from specialist flint crushers. The early flint mills were either wind or water driven and abundant remains of the water driven mills can be seen in the Churnet valley. Cheddleton flint mill has been preserved as a museum and is being restored. By 1782 Josiah Spode had erected a steam engine to crush flints. He was quickly followed by Wedgwood and more gradually by other manufacturers.

The next processes to be mechanized were clay mixing and colour grinding. These, however, were only preliminaries. The first application of power to a manufacturing process seems to have been to the throwers' and turners' wheels.

Pottery develops

As the pottery industry developed and the advantages of factory production became apparent, master potters began to seek partners in order to finance their transfer to the factory system. Josiah Wedgwood, for instance, had several short-lived partnerships before he commenced business with Thomas Bentley at Etruria. Wedgwood planned his new pottery beside the Trent and Mersey Canal and separated the manufacture of useful wares from ornamental wares. At all stages he maintained close contact with his architect, Pickford of Derby. The elevation of the works facing the canal was of classical design with a *cupola* on the roof. But Wedgwood's plans extended beyond the design of a factory and his country house on the hill – he also built a complete township. Much of this has now been demolished but the chapel and a few houses remain.

The finest nineteenth century Georgian facade is that of John Aynsley's pottery in Sutherland Road, Longton, which dates from 1861. It is the usual three storeys high, with a pediment over the central part containing a venetian window. It reflects the isolation from new architectural ideas.

Behind the elegant front elevation all was functional. Single and two storey workshops were ranged around the yard with the *hovels* (kilns) in the centre. There were basically two types of hovel – the typical "bottle oven" and the enamelling kilns, which were much slimmer with taller chimneys protruding from the top. Examples can be seen at the Gladstone Pottery, Longton, which is the proposed Potteries museum.

Although Etruria was a model for the large firm, there were many smaller works which changed little from the courtyard developments behind the master potter's house. Garfield Pottery in Baker Street, Longton, is just one example.

In 1750 the Derby Pottery Company was founded

Below John Aynsley built this pottery at Longton, in Staffordshire, in 1861.

by William Deusbury. In 1773, George II gave the Company the right to the title "Crown Derby" and Queen Victoria granted the prefix "Royal" in 1890. The original company ceased to exist in 1848, but a group of former employees set up in business as the Old Crown Derby China Factory behind a house in King Street. The works were not closed until 1925 and the buildings, with a small kiln, survive today as an antique shop. In 1878, a new firm was established in Derby. It started business in the old workhouse in Osmaston Road and amalgamated with the Old Crown Derby Company. The central part of the Osmaston Road works remains unaltered.

The original Derby company was an important focus for able craftsmen, and several employees later established their own firms. John Coke, for example, started the Pinxton works in 1795. He was joined by William Billingsley from Derby, but the works were short-lived and ceased production in 1818. Considerable parts of the Smalley pottery in Derbyshire can still be seen today.

The Worcester company was started in 1751, by Dr. Wall, in a fine dwelling house backing down to the river. In 1786 an ex-apprentice, Robert Chamberlain, started in business on his own in Diglis – the site now occupied by the Royal Worcester Porcelain factory. In 1840 the two firms amalgamated and between 1852 and about 1860 the works were extensively enlarged. They were rebuilt in red and yellow brick with large segmental arches, largely as they stand at present. A beautiful collection of Worcester pottery can be seen in the Dyson Perrins Museum.

PLACES TO VISIT

Longton, Staffordshire – Aynsley's pottery and Gladstone pottery.

Worcester, Diglis – Royal Worcester pottery.

Glass

By the end of the seventeenth century the Stourbridge area was already noted for its glass industry. This seems to have been established by Protestant glassmakers who settled in the area after fleeing from persecution in France. At this time Stourbridge glass was still chiefly bottle and window glass. The Glass Excise Acts of 1745 and 1777, however, calculated a duty not on the value of the glass but on its weight. This stimulated glass makers in the area to begin the production of high quality, decorated glassware and, by the late eighteenth century, the area was noted for its crystal glass.

The large glass cone, resembling a pottery kiln, is thought to have been introduced into the district sometime prior to 1750, although some kind of smaller cone was probably used earlier. The glass works, like a pottery, was built around a courtyard near the master manufacturer's house. There has been much demolition, but from old billheads and advertisements it can be seen that the exterior of the glass works did not receive the same elaborate architectural treatment as some potteries. A cone has been preserved at the Stuart Crystal Works and a glass museum has been established at Brierley Hill, but the industry is very inadequately recorded.

By the late eighteenth century large glassmaking concerns, operated by merchant manufacturers, had emerged. As in the pottery industry, some of the merchant manufacturers had wide ranging business and social connections. Hill and Waldron of Coalbournhill, for example, were described in 1789 as bankers and glass manufacturers. By 1809 the Hill family had interests in clay mining, brick works, nails, scythes and knives. James Keir, a member of the Birmingham *Lunar Society*, was associated with Holloway End Glasshouse and it is probable that he carried out some of his scientific experiments there. There were also several

PLACES TO VISIT

Brierley Hill, Staffordshire – glass museum.

Wordsley, Brierley Hill – Stuart Crystal glass cone.

links with the Bristol glass trade and some partners had financial interests in works at both places.

The glass tax was much reduced in 1836 and finally abolished in 1845. This led to a great expansion of the glass industry in the Stourbridge area and some large new works were established. Birmingham became an important centre of the industry and Chance's Birmingham works supplied the glass for the Crystal Palace. Early plans of Chance's works still exist and there is also some photographic record. But the glass industry as a whole has until recently received scant attention from historians.

Below Aston Flint Glass Works, near Birmingham, were situated on the banks of a canal. They were owned by B. & W. Gibbins.

Food

In the Industrial Revolution, almost every village had its country corn mill which contained two or three pairs of milling stones. These were simple wind and water mills, whose design had changed little during the preceding two hundred years. There were three basic types of wind mill, which were distinguished by their body structure. The oldest was the post mill. This consisted of a small timber body, containing the milling stones and rotated on an upright post in order to be able to turn the sails into the wind. Often the timber post was protected by masonry to prevent rotting. A fine post mill – the Cat and Fiddle mill – has been preserved near Derby, and Danzey Green post mill has been re-erected at Avoncroft Museum of Buildings. The tower mill was a brick or stone structure, usually two or more storeys high, with a rotating cap on to which the sails were fixed. This cap could be turned by a long tail pole, or by means of an automatic fan tail. The smock mill, less common in the Midlands and so called because its timber superstructure resembled a farmer's smock, was a modified tower mill. By far the most unusual tower mill is Chesterton Mill, preserved and restored by Warwickshire County Council. With its arcaded circular base and small body, it is thought to have been built as an observatory and subsequently converted.

There are abundant remains of water mills in the rural parts of the Midlands. One of the most complete is Charlcot Mill, in Warwickshire, which is part of the Lucy estate. Billing Mill, in Northamptonshire, is a nineteenth century building and is now part of Billing Aquadrome. It has been restored and is open to the public. There is also a mill museum in the Midlands – Sarehole Mill, in Birmingham. This was the last working water mill in the town and has been restored by the City Museum.

The industrial towns were supplied with flour by the

> **PLACES TO VISIT**
>
> **Dale Abbey, Derbyshire –**
> **Cat and Fiddle windmill.**
>
> **Avoncroft Museum,**
> **Bromsgrove – Danzey Green**
> **windmill.**
>
> **Birmingham, Hall Green –**
> **Sarehole Mill Museum.**

larger merchant corn mills, which were first built in the late eighteenth century. The first of these was the steam-driven Birmingham Union Mill, built during the food shortages of the 1790s. A similar mill was built in Wolverhampton in 1812 and, by the mid-nineteenth century, there were at least four large steam corn mills in Birmingham. There were also important mills in Stratford, Bridgnorth and Nuneaton. The merchant millers bought grain, ground it, and sold it to the public. The country millers, on the other hand, frequently ground customers' grain, taking their payment in grain or charging a fee per bushel. Milling later became a port industry and few of the large urban steam mills survive.

Right The sails of a windmill crash to the ground after being struck by lightning during a thunderstorm in 1852.

Brewing

PLACES TO VISIT

Burton-on-Trent – many nineteenth century maltings and breweries.

Broad Street, Birmingham – brewery.

In the eighteenth century, a great deal of ale was "home brewed" by small licensed victuallers. There are still a couple in the Black Country, one being at The Delph. But in the growing industrial towns larger breweries were established – like the Birmingham Brewery, the Phoenix Brewery in Birmingham and Green's Brewery in Nottingham. These were built on a courtyard plan, with *coopers'* workshops and extensive stabling for the large, powerful horses besides the brewing buildings. Derelict nineteenth century breweries can be seen in a number of Midlands towns. They are usually narrow, tower-like, rectangular constructions which protrude above the other buildings in the area. One was used quite recently as a store, by Coventry Museum. With the rise of breweries in Burton-on-Trent, a number of smaller brewers went out of business while others were absorbed by the large Burton companies.

Brewing did not commence on a large scale in Burton until after 1839, when the railway line to Derby was opened. This was because the great markets of the

Above An early drawing of Broad Street Brewery in Birmingham.

industrial Midlands were difficult to reach without the railway. The output of Burton breweries now rapidly increased – Bass Brewery increased its output from 10,000 barrels a year in 1831 to 1,500,000 by 1890, when it was the largest in the country.

London water was less suited to the production of pale ale than Burton water and many London breweries established branches in Burton. Ind Coope came from Romford in 1858, followed by Truman, Hanbury and Buxton in 1873. Charringtons arrived in 1875 and Manns followed later still. Courage's, another London company, contracted a supply of bitter beer from Flowers of Stratford-on-Avon. Flowers brewery has recently been demolished, but Burton's skyline is dominated by the pyramid-shaped, malt kilns and the tall tower blocks of massive nineteenth century breweries.

Manufacturers' Houses – Town houses

The late eighteenth or early nineteenth century master manufacturer, when he first started in business, often lived in a house adjoining or near his workshop, mill or factory. This was chiefly so that he could effectively supervize the works. It also meant, particularly in the case of the town manufacturer, that he only had to purchase one piece of land at a time when land prices and building costs were tending to rise.

This was a very satisfactory arrangement in the industries in which workshops were arranged on a courtyard plan. Many Birmingham button and buckle manufacturers, for example, and Stafford shoe manufacturers, lived in houses which fronted the street while the workshops were ranged around the yard to the rear. Sometimes labourers' dwellings were also built in the courtyard. The courtyard plan developed in a number of industries that required little motive power at first – notably potteries, breweries, and glassworks.

If the business prospered, the manufacturer moved to some fashionable quarter of the town. He purchased a fine house, similar to those favoured by wealthy merchants and bankers, with whom he now mixed socially. In 1762, a visitor to Birmingham described the houses in Temple Row, which faced St. Philips Church (now the cathedral), as "lofty, elegant . . . and inhabited by people of Fortune, who are great wholesale Dealers in the Manufactures of this Town (particularly Mr. Thomas Tipping whose father Mr. Walter Tipping (a founder and merchant) has been known to send away a Waggon-Load of what are called Jew's-Harps at a time.) . . . and this is the highest and genteelest Part of the Town of Birmingham." When Newhall Street was built the wealthy button makers, jewellers and other toy makers moved to the fine, double-fronted three storey brick houses. These had parapets, stone dressings

PLACES TO VISIT

Birmingham – streets by the cathedral, such as Temple Row (merchants' houses).

Low Pavement, Nottingham – houses.

Stafford – Chetwynd House.

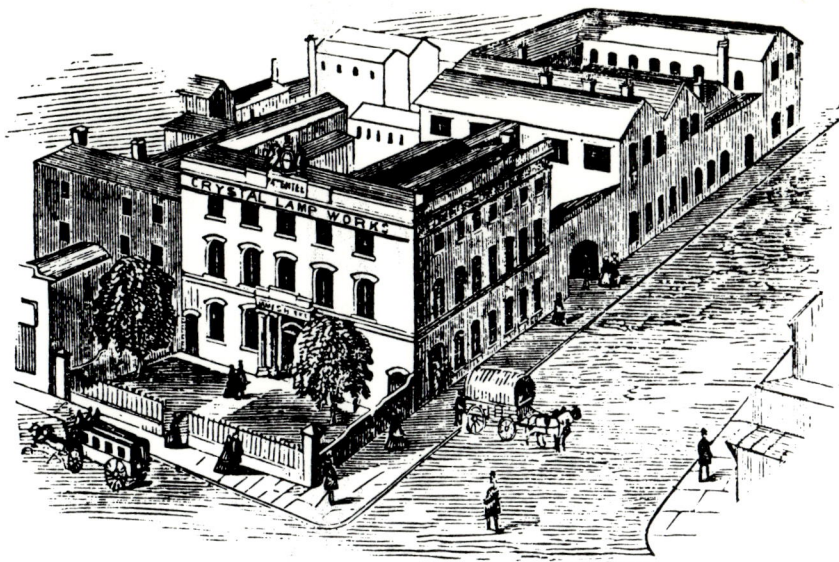

Above A manufacturer's house, with workshops behind, in Birmingham's Great Hampton Street.

and elegant doorways. In nearly every case they had their workshops and warehouses at the back. In 1803, when one of these houses was offered for sale, it was described as . . . "An elegant Mansion . . . built in a remarkably substantial Manner, and fitted up in the best Style, with an elegant Mahogany Staircase, Mahogany Doors, Marble Chimney Pieces, etc., in all the Principal Rooms . . . a truly compleat and eligible Residence for a Professional Gentleman, as well as for a Genteel Family, either in the Mercantile or Manufacturing Line." Behind the house there was "a Range of Warehouses, Compting House, and entire Yard . . . all enclosed by Brick Walls."

Wealthy Nottingham merchant manufacturers and merchant hosiers lived in similar Georgian houses in Low Pavement and Castle Gate. In Leicester, New Walk was favoured by merchant hosiers. And William Horton, the Stafford shoemaker, built a factory behind his fine home – Chetwynd House, which is now the post office.

Country houses

The country manufacturer, whose works were located in a river valley or near supplies of minerals, often lived at first in the "millhouse" by the works. This, like Rock House, Arkwright's first house at Cromford, was usually quite small and unpretentious. Peel House, built near Peel's cotton mills at Burton-on-Trent, is plainer than the town houses of many Birmingham jewellers. Jedediah Strutt, Arkwright's partner, built Milford House, near Milford Mills. This was a somewhat larger classical building, but was nevertheless a plain house.

If the enterprise was successful, managers were trained to supervize the day to day running of the works and the master manufacturer moved to a rather larger, grander house. He left his former home for the use of a manager or trusted foreman. The second house, if built in a town or on the edge of a town, tended to be more ornate and sometimes a little larger than the first. The interior of John Wilkinson's house at Broseley, Shropshire, was designed by Thomas Farnolls Pritchard, the Shropshire architect. William Strutt moved to St. Helens House in King Street, Derby, and one manufacturer built himself a castle.

The building or purchase of a second house represented the enlargement or consolidation of an estate. Arkwright, for example, built Willersley Castle at Cromford, the Strutts built Bridge Hill House at Belper (now demolished), Josiah Wedgwood settled at Etruria and Matthew Boulton at Soho. In 1758 Sampson Lloyd, the Birmingham merchant and banker, built Farm. This was a well-proportioned, small brick country house, set in parkland and approached by a fine avenue of trees. It still survives amidst a sea of Victorian villas which are in varying stages of decay. The Taylors, banking partners of the Lloyds as well as toy manufacturers, purchased Moseley Hall. They rebuilt it in Georgian style, in 1791, after it had been burned in the

PLACES TO VISIT

King Street, Derby – St. Helens House.

Milford House, Derbyshire.

Halesowen, Worcestershire – Corngreaves Hall.

88

Birmingham Riots. The Galtons, Birmingham gun makers, owned several minor country houses – including Warley Hall. Josiah Spode built The Mount on the edge of Burslem. And the Attwood family, metal manufacturers, merchants and bankers, built Corngreaves Hall, near Halesowen.

The successful Victorian manufacturer could build himself a grand town villa. Malvern House in Mapperley Road, Nottingham, and some of the Burton brewers' houses are good examples. But the enormous Victorian country house was beyond the means of all but the very wealthiest. Nottingham hosiery provided the money for the Morleys to build Breadsall Priory, in 1861; beer produced Byrkley Lodge, near Burton, for Hamar Bass in 1887–89; cotton produced The Heath House at Tean, in Staffordshire, built for John Burton Philips between 1836 and 1840; and Droitwich salt paid for the extravagant Chateau Impney which was built between 1869 and 1875 for John Corbett.

Below Corngreaves Hall was the home of the Attwood family, who were metal merchants, manufacturers and bankers.

The grander homes

The building of a larger, grander house posed particular problems for the late eighteenth and early nineteenth century manufacturer. While a more modest house might attract only a passing comment, the larger house more openly proclaimed its builder's taste – or lack of it. For this reason a number of manufacturers trod warily, making discreet enquiries about the most recent and fashionable architectural trends. They were in something of a predicament, for there were at the time two opposing architectural styles in country house building. One was classical and regular, the other gothic and irregular. Since an acceptable classical country house could be built by obeying a set of rules, the majority of manufacturers played safe and adopted this style. It had after all, as Boulton was quick to remark, stood the test of time.

Few Midlands manufacturers could afford, or had the necessary knowledge, to choose an architect of the first rank. Matthew Boulton, who employed both James and Samuel Wyatt to enlarge and remodel Soho House, was an exception, and most wealthy manufacturers employed local architects. Josiah Wedgwood, for example, hired Joseph Pickford of Derby to design Etruria Hall in 1768. This was a larger house than Boulton's. It had a three storey, pedimented block

Left Willersley Castle was built for Richard Arkwright, but he died before it was ready for occupation.

Right Etruria Hall was the home of Josiah Wedgwood. The house still stands, but it has been altered to some extent.

flanked on either side by two storey blocks. Arkwright employed an almost totally unknown architect from London, William Thomas, and his was the most ambitious scheme of all. £3,000 was spent on clearing the site and Thomas was commissioned to design a gothic castle. Willersley Castle is classical in plan (a central block flanked by two smaller ones), built in the battlemented gothic fashion outside and decorated in the Adam style inside. A visitor to the house just after its completion called it "an effort of inconvenient ill-taste."

Many of these grand houses still survive. Many remain to be discovered. They have been ignored by architectural writers because they are not always fine pieces of architecture – they are sometimes insignificant, sometimes ugly. But by investigating manufacturers' houses, as well as the factories, workshops and workers' housing, we get a broader, clearer picture of industrial life in the eighteenth and nineteenth centuries.

PLACES TO VISIT

Cromford, Derbyshire –
Willersley Castle.

Etruria Hall, Staffordshire.

Glossary

ADIT TAILS The point of exit of an underground drainage channel.

BALER A person who emptied the buckets in the primitive mine drainage system which involved a chain of buckets.

BAG HOSIER A small country hosier who usually began in business as the agent of a town merchant hosier.

BISCUIT WARE Pottery that has had one firing but has not been glazed.

BELL PITS Coal or ore pits where the minerals were mined outwards from a shallow vertical shaft, thus forming the shape of a bell.

BUTTY SYSTEM A system of sub-contracting in the coal mining industry, practiced extensively in south Staffordshire.

BUDDLE A circular stone structure used for washing ore.

COE A Derbyshire lead miner's hut.

COOPER A maker of barrels.

CUPOLA A curved or domed structure on a roof.

DOUBLER A person who doubled (laid) threads of silk together before they were twisted to form a usable yarn.

ENCAUSTIC TILE A decorated, coloured tile used in flooring and wall decoration.

FLATTED FACTORY A factory which houses a number of separate small firms.

FLUE A channel for carrying away the noxious fumes produced in smelting.

FUSTIAN A fabric made of linen or wool and cotton.

GIN A series of simple gears used to pump out mines, wind up coal and ore and provide rotary motion in early factories. It was usually powered by animals.

HOVEL The brick structure which gives the characteristic bottle shape to a pottery kiln.

JIGGING MACHINE A kind of sieve for washing ore.

KIBBLE A pan or basket in which coal or ore were raised

to the surface.

LONGWALL SYSTEM A method of mining in which the whole face is opened up in one operation and the worked out part is filled in with waste.

LUNAR SOCIETY A philosophical society founded in Birmingham towards the end of the eighteenth century. Membership was by invitation and included James Watt, Matthew Boulton and Josiah Wedgwood.

OLIVER A foot operated hammer with a light timber pole acting as a spring.

PEDIMENT A triangular, ornamental gable over some central projecting bays of a building. Also a triangular head to windows or doors.

PILLAR AND STALL A method of mining in which the coal face is opened up in squares, leaving sections of the face intact to hold up the roof.

POINT NET MACHINE A modified stocking frame, used for making net.

PIG IRON Iron tapped from the blast furnace and run into a casting bed. This bed consisted of a central channel with smaller ones leading off it and was said to resemble a mother sow with her piglets.

REVERBERATORY FURNACE A smelting furnace in which the fuel and the ore were kept separate. This prevented the metals from picking up impurities from the coal.

SOUGH A channel constructed to carry water from a mine.

SPINDLE The mechanism on a spinning machine onto which the spun thread is wound.

SPRING POLE A flexible pole used as a spring in an oliver hammer.

STEVENGRAPH A picture, frequently topical, made of woven silk.

TOMMY A small, foot-operated hammer with a strong metal spring instead of a pole.

VENETIAN WINDOW A set of three panes, the central one larger than those to either side, under a single head.

Further Reading

S. D. Chapman, *The Early Factory Masters* (David & Charles, 1967).

F. Nixon, *Industrial Archaeology of Derbyshire* (David & Charles, 1969).

J. Prest, *The Industrial Revolution in Coventry* (Oxford University Press, 1960).

T. J. Raybould, *The Economic Emergence of the Black Country. . . .* (David & Charles, 1973).

D. Smith, *Industrial Archaeology of the East Midlands* (David & Charles, 1965).

J. Tann, *The Development of the Factory* (Cornmarket Press, 1970).

B. Trinder, *Shropshire in the Industrial Revolution* (Phillimore, 1973).

M. Albutt & F. Brook, "The South Shropshire Lead Mines," *Industrial Archaeology,* 10, 1973.

J. N. Bartlett, "The Mechanization of the Kidderminster Carpet Industry," *Business History,* 9, 1967.

R. A. Church, "Messrs. Gotch and Sons and the Rise of the Kettering Footwear Industry," *Business History,* 8, 1966.

N. McKendrick, "Josiah Wedgwood and Thomas Bentley. . . ." *Transactions of the Royal Historical Society,* 14, 1964.

N. Mutton, "Eardington Forges and Canal Tunnel," *Industrial Archaeology,* 7, 1970.

B. C. G. Nokes, "John English of Feckenham, Needle Manufacturer," *Business History,* 11, 1969.

D. M. Smith, "Birmingham's Gun Quarter and its Workshops," *Business History,* 9, 1967.

G. H. Starmer, "Northamptonshire Wind and Water Mills," *Bulletin of Industrial Archaeology* C.B.A. Group, 9th April 1970.

J. Tann, "Richard Arkwright and Technology," *History,* 1973.

R. Wailes, "Water Driven Mills for Grinding Stone," *Transactions Newcomen Society,* 39, 1966–67.

Index

Picture Credits

The Publishers wish to thank the following for their kind permission to reproduce copyright illustrations on the pages mentioned: W. & T. Avery Ltd., 14–15, 25 (bottom); Birmingham Public Libraries, 19; Geoffrey Booth, jacket, 9, 11, 16–17, 18–19, 19, 25 (top), 27, 35, 36, 39, 43, 45, 47, 49, 50–51, 58–59, 66, 67, 68–69, 70–71, 71, 73, 74, 75, 76–77, 77, 78–79, 81, 85, 87, 89, 90, 91; F. Brook, 22–23, 23; Inga Bulman, 29, 30–31, 33; H. M. Fitzroy-Newdigate, 15; Northampton Museum and Art Gallery, 65. Other Illustrations appearing in this book are the property of the Wayland Picture Library.